Pr

HIDDEN

in

PLAIN SIGHT

"Janis Owens's first foray into nonfiction writing is an unqualified success. Owens uses her writing and detective skills to tell the story of a largely forgotten lynching in her adopted home near Gainesville, Florida. *Hidden in Plain Sight* is a fine work of history. It is a precious gift to a state and a nation prone to forgetfulness."

—James M. Denham

Professor of History and Director, Lawton Chiles Center for Florida History, Florida Southern College

"*Hidden in Plain Sight* is both a crime scene investigation and meticulously researched diagnosis of a century-old murder, solved through real-time detective work. This book should become standard reading for Florida history and university-level American history courses. Know that this is not another contrived entry into the carefully cleaned and politically correct history we've come to know, where polished textbook chapters gloss over the jagged edges of civilization, bolstering the glimmer of celebrated explorers. This important work instead unearths the buried truth so that we are forced to see the ugliness along the way—the inhumane way people persecuted others to rise above them."

—Dana Ste. Claire

Professional archaeologist and museum designer, Heritage Cultural Services, LLC, Author of *Cracker: Cracker Culture in Florida History*.

"Hidden in Plain Sight: A History of the Newberry Lynching of 1916 is the definitive accounting of the Newberry massacre. The historical documentation is thorough and much of it is new. The writing is exquisite, and contributes in major ways, among the most important being the establishment of a credible timeline and additional evidence. The coverage brings the time period to light in ways that are as authentic as I have ever read. It should be recognized as the most reliable document to date on the Newberry event."

—Dr. Marvin Dunn
Florida Historian, Author of *A History of Florida Through Black Eyes*

"Master storyteller and Florida historian Janis Owens has written a powerful and soul-stirring account of dark days in North Florida. *Hidden in Plain Sight: A History of the Newberry Mass Lynching of 1916* is an important book that reminds us if history is kept secret, societal wounds fester and atrocities are likely to be repeated. This page-turning book is a must read for anyone who wants to better understand the haunting, generational scars of racism and injustice on the rural South. With an eye toward remembrance, Owens beautifully reminds the reader that the first step toward healing is to bear witness to the truth."

—Michael Morris
Author of *A Place Called Wiregrass, Slow Way Home,* and *Man in the Blue Moon*

Hidden in Plain Sight:

A History of the Newberry Mass Lynching of 1916

By Janis Owens

© Copyright 2021 Janis Owens

ISBN 978-1-64663-368-5

Published by

köehlerbooks™

3705 Shore Drive
Virginia Beach, VA 23455
800–435–4811
www.koehlerbooks.com

HIDDEN

in

PLAIN SIGHT

A History of the Newberry Mass Lynching of 1916

Janis Owens

VIRGINIA BEACH
CAPE CHARLES

For Patricia Hilliard-Nunn,
who embodied the passion and power of Sankofa.

Table of Contents

"It may be a good thing to forget and forgive; but it is altogether too easy a trick to forget and be forgiven."

—G. K. Chesterton

PREFACE

A t two a.m. on August 17, 1916, three men engaged in a gun battle in a vacant tenant shack in the cut-over pine barrens of Western Alachua County, nine miles west of Gainesville. Two of the men were white: George Wynne, a bachelor and seasoned deputy sheriff, and Lem Harris, a popular young pharmacist from nearby Newberry, who was recently married and had an infant son. The Black man, Boisy Long, was a farmer and father of three.

Deputy Wynne died the following morning from bullet wounds to his liver and lungs. His death sparked a murderous rampage that resulted in the vigilante lynching of six Blacks—possibly more. Two of those hanged were women, and a third who was heavily pregnant was brutalized. All of the Black victims were connected by blood, marriage or kinship to Boisy, who was captured, tried and then hanged several weeks later.

Thousands of spectators assembled at the mass lynching site to gawk and celebrate as if at a country fair. Several local dignitaries were surely among them, perhaps even the man who would become Florida's next governor. Young children were said to have pushed the dangling corpses like swings at a playground. After the bodies were cut down, they were dumped like sacks on the ground as witnesses and perpetrators stood over them posing for photographers.

There are varying accounts of the circumstances that brought Long and the two white men to confrontation at such an odd hour of the night, and even more debate over who fired the first shot—the deputy, the pharmacist, or Boisy Long. What is indisputable is that the brief flare of gunfire—six rapid shots in the dark—sparked an American tragedy of uncommon proportions, one shameful in its brutality and doubly shameful in that it's never merited more than a footnote in Florida history, though the larger community and the family of Deputy Wynne have been preserved down to the smallest nail and chicken coop at their family farm, now known as Dudley State Park.

Oaths of silence were taken that bloody weekend in 1916 and kept so securely that even a century later, the most enduring remembrance of the violence is an oak grove on the east end of Newberry that for over a hundred years has been called, casually and without regret, "Lynch Hammock."

The history of the hammock and the names of those who were murdered that frantic, bloody weekend were very nearly lost to history. Among the confirmed dead were Deputy George Wynne; James Dennis; Reverend J. J. "Josh" Baskins; Gilbert Dennis; Andrew McHenry; Mary Dennis; Stella Young. Names of other victims might someday be added to the list of the murdered. According to the oral history of Jonesville—and even a photograph of the day—a longer count could be made.[1]

---

1   Maria Dennis and Dick Johnson are also possible victims. According to Frank Dudley, Maria Dennis was not lynched because she was pregnant. Her name has not been located on further censuses, and her true fate is unclear. Newberrian Mary Welch said that a man named Dick Johnson also died that weekend, captured by the mob as he drove home in his buggy. (Claudia Adrien, "The Newberry Six," *Gainesville Sun*, Sep. 4, 2005)

Myrtle Dudley said that three Black men were buried in the banks of the railroad between "here and Gainesville." Those bodies have never been found. (Myrtle Dudley, Oral History Interview with Lisa Heard, February 25, 1992, pg. 10, Samuel Proctor Oral History Program Collection, P.K. Yonge Library of Florida History, University of Florida.)

Another victim in Jacksonville is mentioned in the *Ocala Evening Star*, August 19, 1916. That victim was not named, but was possibly part of the arrests made by Ham Dowling near Mayport on August 17.

These are the *known* casualties, those deaths that were documented in some form or fashion in newspapers, first-source witnesses, and court records of the day. The details of their last moments on earth were ignored, garbled, or intentionally denied. It is only with a close examination of the fading ink of history, along with oral history and a handful of first-hand testimony, that we can establish the circumstances of their final moments on earth.

Deputy Wynne died in the back seat of a borrowed Model-T Ford on the morning of August 18th, while being rushed to a waiting train in Waldo, Florida, in a futile attempt to get him to the hospital in Jacksonville for an operation that might save his life. James Dennis died at ten that same morning after being abducted at his home. He was shot in the back with a double-barreled shotgun by a vengeful member of a mob, reportedly a sworn deputy. The Reverend J. J. Baskins was returning home from the market in Newberry later in the day when he was caught by the same mob and hanged. James Dennis' brother, Gilbert, his sister Mary, his in-laws Andrew McHenry and Boisy Long's wife, Stella Young Long, were systematically murdered at two o'clock in the morning of August 19, on the one-day anniversary of Deputy Wynne's shooting.

The five Blacks lynched together were hanged two miles east of downtown Newberry at the old picnic grounds, in an oak hammock with a sink that created a natural amphitheater, that had become popular for both lynch parties and political speeches. The mob, later described by an eyewitness as two hundred of "the best men in the district," chose the site for its close proximity to the highway, as the lynching of J. J. Baskins, Andrew McHenry, Albert Dennis, Mary Dennis and Stella Young was a spectacle lynching, meant for public consumption.

So intent was the mob that the corpses be publicly displayed that two guards were posted to make sure they weren't immediately cut down, but left to hang until mid-afternoon in the pitiless Florida sun. On Saturday morning, August 18, 1916, the Old Gainesville Highway that lead west to Newberry—a rutted hard-rock road more suited to cattle drives than automobiles—was overrun by a steady stream of enthusiastic tourists.

Men, women, and not a few children came from all over the county, and numbered in the thousands to gather at the old picnic grounds and witness the mob's handiwork—the piteous, decaying corpses of a Methodist preacher, two brothers, their sister and her sister-in-law.

INDEPENDENT OF THE WORLD

Figure 1. Finley's Map of Florida 1827.
Courtesy of Florida Memory

Alachua is one of the older counties in Florida, created by the Florida territorial government in 1824, twenty-one years before Florida achieved statehood. Tucked securely into North Florida, the landmass of the original county was considerably larger than it is today. Long and narrow, it was bounded by the Georgia state line to the north, the Suwannee River to the west, and an ungainly dogleg to the south that stretched to the gulf at Charlotte Harbor.

The Suwannee marks the boundary of West and East Florida, and Alachua made up a good slice of East Florida so long that the topography changes from top to bottom. The Georgia side of the county was more attached to the plantation district of Middle Florida, while the southern end was more palmetto than live oak, still inhabited by the Seminole and their allies.

On early maps the central part of the sprawling county was described as high rolling pine, or less attractively, as pine barrens, and closer to the coast, the flatwoods. The aquifer was higher then, bursting the seams of the fragile limestone to flow aboveground in shallow ponds and sinks so wide that when the water line withdrew, the lakes became prairies.

Wildlife was abundant, and indigenous tribes had lived on the banks of the springs and gulf of Alachua County for eons. The tribes included the Timucuan, and further east, the Potanom. The very name, *Alachua,* was a derivation of a Muskogee word for sinkhole, or big jug.

By the time Florida gained statehood in 1845, the remnant aboriginal tribes had long been extinguished by European conquest and even more deadly, European disease. Even the Spanish, who'd been in Florida since the 1500s, who'd established missions along the Santa Fe River and at San Felasco, and vast cattle ranching on the prairie at Arredondo, were mostly gone. The county's most recent inhabitants, the Seminole, had been driven south of Fort King by the ongoing action of the Second Seminole War.

The remaining population of Alachua County was sparse, hardy, and ethnically diverse. They were a melting pot of the descendants of the Indians, Europeans, and Africans who'd survived brutal wars, brutal heat and a host of feared diseases to eke out a hardscrabble life in the trackless, and nearly lawless wilderness.

In 1842, Congress opened the floodgates to immigration to the area when it passed the Armed Occupation and Settlement Act for the express purpose of luring white settlers to the area. The qualifications of the Act were simple: anyone who built a home, cultivated five acres, and promised to resist the Seminole for five years received 160 acres of land and rations for a year from the federal government.

The offer of free land was, as always, enticing, and yeomen farmers from across the South began a steady trek to East Florida, along with cotton planters from Georgia and the Lowcountry of South Carolina, whose cotton plantations had depleted the land for other farming. The climate and soil of East Florida wasn't considered as lush as the red dirt of the plantation belt of Middle Florida, but it had been found to be amendable to growing Sea Island cotton, a long-strand cotton that brought a premium price at market.

A South Carolina planter, overseer and cattleman named Phillip B. H. Dudley was one of those immigrants, arriving in Alachua County in the early 1850s.

Figure 2. Phillip Benjamin Harvey Dudley, 1870. Courtesy Florida Memory

Born outside of Charleston in 1818, Dudley had begun his working life as an accountant and overseer of enslaved laborers at the Legare Plantation in St. Johns, South Carolina. He later owned his own plantation, possibly from his wife's family, called Walnut Hill.[2] When Dudley first came to Florida he worked in the lucrative cattle trade, and as an overseer of a two hundred-slave cotton plantation in the area of Fort Clarke.[3]

---

2 Ben Pickard with Sally Morrison, *Dudley Farm, A History of Florida Farm Life*, Alachua Press, 2003
3 Ibid

Converting the high rolling pine barrens of Western Alachua County into viable cotton land required hard, relentless labor and a cheap supply of it, which South Carolina planters like Dudley introduced to the East Florida wilderness in the form of enslaved Black labor. As an overseer, Dudley's job was to extract labor from the plantation owner's slaves. Overseers were sometimes referred to as *drivers*, which was an apt description of their job—to drive their enslaved laborers, men, women, and children, to long hours, faster work and higher production.

Overseers were valued for their toughness, their ability to maintain order, and their efficiency in administering rigid, violent discipline to their master's slaves. Punishment was harsh and could include whipping, confinement in sweat boxes, branding, mutilation, or being sold on the auction block.[4] There is no written record of P. B. H. Dudley's precise treatment of the enslaved laborers under his management, but his rapid rise from accountant, to overseer, to plantation owner suggests that he was effective in the work of managing enslaved laborers, which would have included a willingness to administer brutal intimidation and punishment.

Dudley prospered in central Alachua County, accumulating his own slaves and land in the area of Archer and Arredondo. He served as a trustee for the fledgling Alachua County school board, and worked for the county road commission. His job with the highway commission was similar to his work on the plantation. As an overseer, he was paid to oversee enslaved Blacks in the backbreaking labor of hacking a primitive highway through the dense scrub, swamp and pine of Western Alachua County between Archer and the county seat at Newnansville. It was in his position as a road commissioner that Dudley found three hundred choice acres of high rolling pine and hammock six miles west of Fort Clarke, where he planned to establish his own Florida plantation.

---

4   Larry E. Rivers, *Slavery in Florida: Territorial Days to Emancipation,* University Press of Florida, 2000

On the 1860 federal census, Dudley was listed as living on his new property with his wife, Mary, and three children—Virginia, Ben and Joanna—with his post office listed as Archer.[5] He had nine hundred sixty acres and thirty enslaved laborers,[6] making him one of the more prominent planters in Alachua County.

The names of enslaved laborers were not listed on the census, but age, sex and race are recorded. On the Federal Slave Schedule, taken July 6, 1860, Dudley owned six female enslaved laborers, three of whom were age eighteen. The rest were male laborers and children ranging in age from age eight to eighty-two.

All thirty of the Dudley slaves were listed as mulatto, which was unusual at the time, but not unknown. Some Florida slaveowners, such as Duval County's Zephaniah Kingsley Jr., were known to prefer mixed race, then called mulatto slaves.[7] Some of Kingsley's mixed race slaves were his own children, a product of forced slave concubinage, which was a common practice of the day. It is possible that Dudley, like Kingsley, bred his own enslaved women, though unlike Kingsley, Dudley was never known to have freed or acknowledged any slave mistresses or children.

The house that P. B. H. Dudley's slaves built on his Gainesville Road property was by modern standards primitive; by frontier standards wholly adequate; a double-pen dog trot—basically two rooms covered by a single roof with a breezeway between—that was sufficient for homestead. Dudley's plans to build a larger, Georgian-style plantation house were interrupted by Florida's secession from the Union in 1861, which Dudley, a slaveowner and ardent secessionist, fully supported. There has been some debate between Florida historians and local Black historians as to whether Dudley's farm had its genesis as a slave plantation, or a more simple dirt

---

5   J. J. Jones, his son-in-law, is listed as a neighbor, indicating he'd moved to his new property by 1860.
6   ibid
7   Daniel L. Schafer, *Zephaniah Kingsley Jr. and the Atlantic World: Slave Trader, Plantation Owner, Emancipator,* University of Florida Presses, 2013

farm, owing to the fact that Dudley's plantation house was built after 1865.

Myrtle Dudley confirms that enslaved Black laborers built his original dog-trot structure on the Old Gainesville Road, and has recollections of slaves who lived on the property, including the family of Becky Perkins, who are reflected on the federal census. Before and after the Civil War, both P. B. H. Dudley and his son Ben were referred to in local newspapers as "prominent planters," and their capital investment in enslaved labor was far more extensive that the more common small-holding dirt farmer. The State of Florida may split hairs on the exact definition of plantation, but P. B. H. Dudley's three hundred acres were bought by a slaveowner, and cleared by his enslaved labor. Had the war not intervened, he would have had them cultivate Sea Island cotton.

True to his South Carolina roots, Dudley was instrumental in establishing Company C, 7th Florida Infantry, CSA, where he served as captain, an honorific that he would carry until his death in 1881.[8] His company saw action in the western theatre, from Chickamauga to Nashville, before he furloughed out in 1863 after a life-threatening bout with dysentery. When he recovered, he returned to action for the final skirmishes in Florida in Olustee, the defense of Gainesville, and the Battle of Otter Creek.[9]

In an oral history taken in 1992, Myrtle Dudley recounted her grandfather's Civil War service: ". . . Grandpa and them hitched up his slaves, got his own slaves up, and was made captain of his own army team, and he went to the War Between the States. He was in the battle at Jacksonville. They tore it all to pieces. He traced it all the way around the coast clear back to over yonder on the coast over there. Then he turned in and come back to where he was at first. He

---

8   ibid
9   Ben Pickard with Sally Morrison, *Dudley Farm, A History of Florida Farm Life*, Alachua Press, 2003

took camp dysentery, and they brought him home in a wagon that [was] padded."[10]

The Confederacy was defeated in 1865, after a harrowing four years that devastated Southern cities and a large area of Georgia and South Carolina, where Sherman torched a wide swath in a ruthless bid to break the Confederates' will.

Western Alachua County was too poorly inhabited to draw the wrath of Union troops, but when the Confederates surrendered in 1865, Dudley and his planter neighbors not only faced the psychological trauma of defeat, but the collapse of the plantation culture and loss of the enslaved Black laborers who had built their East Florida fortunes. These former slaves—now called freedmen— were no longer a commodity that was literally bought and sold to the highest bidder, but instead became a sudden majority population. Until the Compromise of 1877, new freedmen were an active voting block in Alachua County elections.

They were no longer tied to bondage on local plantations, but free to move, which many did, to greater opportunities in the North and West. Other freedmen stayed in the area and worked in the job that slavery had trained them to do well: farming, often for their former owners, in crop-sharing or barter arrangements.

Their new freedom was still a fragile guarantee, as returning ex-Confederates were bitter in loss, and keen to return East Florida to antebellum white supremacy. In the early days of Reconstruction, the freedmen were protected by Union troops, some of them Black, that were garrisoned in Gainesville. They were also supported by the Bureau of Refugees, Freedmen, and Abandoned Lands (commonly called the Freedman Bureau), which was passed by a staunch Republican Congress to help emancipated slaves establish themselves in Reconstruction.

---

10   Myrtle Dudley, Oral History Interview with Lisa Heard, February 25, 1992, pg. 3, Samuel Proctor Oral History Program Collection, P. K. Yonge Library of Florida History, University of Florida.

According to African-American historian Patricia Hilliard-Nunn, Alachua County freedmen took Emancipation seriously. They were well aware that they were the majority voters in a county with a hostile ex-Confederate presence, and "didn't twiddle their thumbs," but worked hard to establish their own communities, building churches and schools, and joining a variety of black fraternal organizations.[11]

On the West end of the county, Greater Liberty Hill (1869), New Zion Methodist (later named Pleasant Plain) (1868), and Fort Clarke Missionary Baptist Church (1867), were founded, to name but a few.[12] Johnson Chestnut, a former slave from Haile Plantation, oversaw the construction of Union Academy in Gainesville, and served on the Gainesville City Commission.

Figure 3. Early Freedman School, before 1880. Courtesy of Alachua County Library

---

11   Patricia Hilliard-Nunn, *Gainesville Sun*, August 9, 2014
12   Lizzie PRB Jenkins, *Alachua County*, *Black American Series*, Arcadia Publishing

The Freedman's Liberty Hill School opened in Rutledge in 1869, as did many smaller black schools in Pinewood and Jonesville. Other black communities did likewise, and by 1883, Carl Webber noted that there were thirty to forty schools for colored children in the county surrounding Gainesville.[13] Many of the schools were supported by Black fraternal organizations. Historian Lizzie PBR Jenkins Robinson notes that organizations such as "Archer Night Riders, Knights of Pythias, and Men of Worth alliance worked to enhance and empower community relations. They addressed each other as 'Sir' and built lasting relationships. It was imperative for them to take care of their own."[14] A Black Jonesville midwife named Matilda Haile joined with other Black women in Jonesville and Rutledge to form The Female Protective Society, a benevolent organization designed to support Black farming families with medical care and funeral costs.

Freedmen in Gainesville and the surrounding communities were able to open their own businesses and homestead their own farms, which were small and self-sufficient for the most part, though Webber noted in 1883 that the largest truck farm in the county was owned by a Black man, Congressman Josiah T. Walls, an educator who farmed a thousand acres on the northern edge of Payne's Prairie.[15]

These ongoing gains were made even as the legal structure of Emancipation was hammered out in the halls of Congress in Washington. In 1866, the Civil Rights Act passed over Andrew Johnson's veto, and the Fourteenth Amendment, which granted former enslaved laborers equal protection under the law, was ratified in 1868. Ex-Confederates bitterly opposed both, but were outvoted in the First Reconstruction Act of 1867, which forced Southern states to ratify the Fourteenth and later the Fifteenth Amendment as a precondition for re-entry into the Union.

The ferocity of the political battles being played out in Congress

---

13   Carl Webber, *Eden of the South*, 1883
14   Lizzie PRB Jenkins, *Black America Series Alachua County Florida*, Arcadia Press
15   Carl Webber, *Eden of the South*, 1883

were mild compared to the incessant guerilla warfare being waged against freedmen in Western Alachua County by area planters and native whites, violence so vicious and immediate that it could be said to be a continuation of the war itself. Myrtle Dudley recalled, "Some of the owners in this community burned everything the niggers had when they were freed. It was pitiful around, and them babies had to eat. They got to where they would come up a work a half a day almost for a piece of bread."[16]

Gainesville Freedman Bureau Chief Leonard G. Dennis testified before Congress in 1872 that eighteen men were murdered in the early years of Reconstruction in Alachua County.[17] Josiah Walls was himself nearly assassinated at a political rally. In 1872, a former Klansman named Frank Meyers testified before Congress of the activities of associated white supremacist organizations. The Ku Klux Klan, as well as the Secret Service Committee and their social arm, the Young Democrats Club, had active organizations in Alachua County. They attacked freedmen and their allies with assassinations, house-burnings, whippings, and one method that would become a symbol of racial terrorism for a century to come—the practice of vigilante lynching.[18]

Broadly defined as "vigilante execution by a mob of more than three people," the practice of lynching was not invented by white men in Reconstruction, but had been a common form of outlaw justice in the United States since the country's inception. There are records of whites lynching whites, Blacks lynching Blacks, and every

16   Myrtle Dudley, Oral History Interview with Lisa Heard, February 25, 1992, pg. 44, Samuel Proctor Oral History Program Collection, P.K. Yonge Library of Florida History, University of Florida.

17   *Report of the Joint Select Committee to Inquire into the Condition of Affairs in the Late Insurrectionary States, made to the two Houses of Congress,* February 19, 1872

18   When pressed for names of the head of the Alachua County Ku Klux Klan, Meyers says he was known to him only as "Doctor Dudley." Whether that name is connected to Captain Dudley is not known. Pg. 160, *Report of the Joint Select Committee to Inquire into the Condition of Affairs in the Late Insurrectionary States, made to the two Houses of Congress,* February 19, 1872

other racial combination in the melting pot of Colonial America. The practice was considered an acceptable form of justice in pioneer regions where courts were seldom in session, and due process not easily accessible. The standard manner of execution in early lynchings was hanging. The rope and noose continue to be the most common symbol of the act, though lynching was accomplished through other means, including gunfire, whippings and even burning at the stake.

In the guerilla warfare of Reconstruction, the extra-legal practice lost its tenuous ties to justice and became a favored instrument of white racial terror, with the predominant instances being Black men lynched for accusations of crimes as serious as murder and as minor as insolence. The Alachua County Historical Commission has set the official count of lynching victims in Alachua County at forty-three and the Jonesville number at fifteen. Both counts are almost surely underreported, as a close reading of the local newspapers and the oral history of the area reveal.

Myrtle Dudley conceded as much when speaking of the fate of Dudley's enslaved laborers, many of whom left after the war, but not all. "A few of those old nigras stayed here," she recalled. "Some of them went to the towns and around different places. You do not know how many of them were killed and just buried, either."[19]

The ongoing racial violence across the South, along with shifting political alliances in Washington, led to the Compromise of 1877, which pulled the last of the occupying Union troops from the South and restored the Old Guard to power in the Florida statehouse. The new order bore great similarity to the Old Order—white ex-Confederates in alliance with big business interests that were pouring into North Florida. Naval stores, lumber concerns, phosphate mining, and road-building had much in common with antebellum plantations—both required a cheap and abundant labor source.

Almost immediately, all Southern states, including Florida, began writing new constitutions that allowed for strict segregation

---

19   ibid

and poll taxes. When Homer Plessy sued in the courts arguing that segregation laws violated the equal protection clause of the Fourteenth Amendment, the US Supreme Court cast the argument aside claiming in *Plessy v. Ferguson* (1896) that a state's police powers allowed them to segregate the races. The court upheld the notion of separate but equal.

Even before these race-restrictive laws—commonly called Jim Crow—went into effect, new labor laws forced freedmen to sign annual labor contracts that curtailed their freedom of movement. Black men could be harshly penalized for abandoning contracts before labor was complete, and were subject to vagrancy laws that gave local sheriffs great leniency in arresting them, often for the purpose of providing bodies to fill the quota of convict leasing contracts between the State of Florida and incoming industries.

The Alachua County freedmen who had continued to farm in chop-sharing or barter arrangements soon found themselves tied to a brutal system of peonage, where land owners would sell tenants the necessary items to make a crop—the seeds, mules, and equipment. They'd expect repayment at harvest in the form of a share of the crop, an exchange that was easily manipulated, as slaves had been forbidden education so freedmen were often illiterate. No matter how skilled they were at farming, freedmen were at the mercy of the landowners who owned the roofs over their heads, and the commissary where they bought their supplies that could set prices to their advantage. Sharecroppers caught in the peonage system seldom cleared enough profit to buy their own property, living lives that were not very far removed from slavery.

***

The legal structure of Jim Crow was firmly in place by the turn of the twentieth century, upheld by state statute and oftentimes administered by capricious vigilante justice, as was the lynching of two young Black men, Manny Price and Rob Scruggs, in Jonesville in 1903. Price was accused of murdering a white man, W. F. Brunson, who worked as an overseer at the Komoko Phosphate Mine, just east of Newberry.

The murder occurred over a dispute connected to a loud poker game, though the details of the encounter changed over the course of the investigation, as crimes that ended in lynchings tended to do. The initial story was that Brunson went to close the noisy game down and was shot. Later news reports said that Price lay in wait for Brunson and assassinated him. Price then escaped for several weeks until he was picked up by the sheriff in Folkston, Georgia, and brought back to Newberry to face charges. He implicated Rob Scruggs as the man who'd given him the gun used to shoot Brunson, an accusation no one seems to have doubted or investigated.

The truth of the accusations was never determined in court because the special deputy who was transferring them from Newberry to stand trial in Gainesville was overtaken by a mob of three hundred. The two Black men were abducted and lynched two miles from town, in an oak-grown hammock that was popular for picnics and lynchings, enough of which that the Black community had lately taken to calling it "Hangman's Island."

Local newspapers reported that after they were hanged, Price and Scruggs' bodies were riddled by bullets.[20] The papers omitted a few less civilized details that were remembered in local oral history— how that the ropes that hung them were kept as souvenirs by the mob leaders who wore them around as neckties in a symbol of laughing contempt. Also omitted was the price the families of the victims paid; their homes were burnt to the ground, and they were run out of town for no other crime than kinship with the accused men.[21]

---

20   "Lynching at Newberry" *Ocala Evening Star*, September 1, 1902; "Price in Prison" *Ocala Evening Star,* September 2, 1902
21   Patricia Hilliard-Nunn, 2013

Local newspapers followed the story closely, reporting details of the initial crime, the accusations, and the lynching itself, taking care to omit the names of the white deputies and the members of the mob, who were local men. There is no mention that they attempted to hide their faces with hoods or disguise, which would have made them easily identified.

In 1908, another well-publicized lynching took place at Hangman's Island when a white man named Jack Long was accused, later thought falsely,[22] of the murder of a well-regarded Jonesville businessman, Elias Sapp. The shooting was thought to be in retaliation for an earlier murder of a kinsman of Long's, but nothing, least of all his guilt, was ever established in court.

On the night of February 9, Long was broken out of the Newberry jail and paraded in a single-file "death march" to Hangman's Island in an elaborate pseudo-legal ceremony, with a "judge," guards, and chance to repent. He was hanged, then his body riddled with bullets.[23]

So common was the lynching of Black men in Western Alachua County that early newspaper reports of Long's lynching incorrectly described him as Black. When he was found to be white, a tongue-in-cheek retraction was offered in the Ocala newspaper, that Long "was a white man instead of a negro. It has come to be natural to infer that anyone lynched in this part of the world is a negro."[24]

The "part of the world" the editor referred to was the West End of Alachua County, that sparsely settled former plantation district, which had earned, even before the Wild West era of phosphate mining, a reputation for hard self-sufficiency in all matters, including vigilante justice. Details of life there between Reconstruction and the arrival of the railroad are hard to come by, though a few insightful descriptions can be found, one in Carl Webber's 1883 real estate tract, *Eden of the South*.

---

22   Untitled article, *The Ocala Evening Star*, February 7, 1908
23   *Gainesville Daily Sun*, "Lynching Occurs at Newberry" February 10, 1908
24   *Ocala Evening Star*, (untitled) February 7, 1908

In it, Alachua County was described in the dreamy, overwrought language of the day as "a spot where man might live and enjoy the bounties of the earth with perfect safety to health, life and happiness, and with commensurate renumeration for the toil of his hands and brain."[25]

Webber was less effusive when describing the West End, a place he deemed ". . . independent of the world, outside their own neighborhood, as it is possible for human beings to be. They raise their own food, make their own clothes, from products raised by their own labor, and think, talk and act as they please in accordance with their own well-regulated social laws."[26]

Webber did not name names, but given the scarcity of population on the West End in 1883, he was almost certainly describing the highly self-sufficient and independent neighborhood of the Dudley Plantation.

---

25   Carl Webber, *Eden of the South*, 1883
26   ibid

Chapter Two

A HELL OF A LIFE

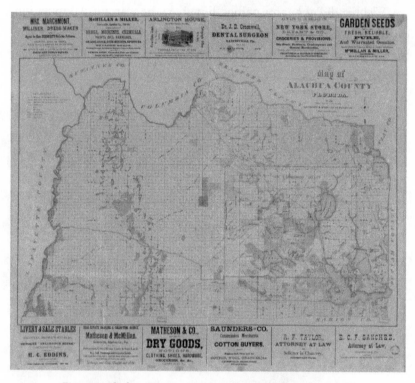

Figure 4. Alachua County, 1880, Dudley noted in pink square[27]

---

27   Matheson & McMillan Publishers. *Map of Alachua County, Florida.* [Gainesville, Florida: Matheson & McMillan Publishers, 188] Map. Retrieved from the Library of Congress, <www.loc.gov/item/2012592398/>.

When Captain Dudley died in 1881, he left his plantation to his only surviving son, Phillip Benjamin Dudley, Jr., who was called Ben. Born in 1852, Ben Dudley came of age while the Captain was off fighting for the Confederacy in the Civil War. Born into a slave-holding family, he would have been well versed in the "well-regulated social laws"[28] that held sway on the West End, including the numerous incidents of racial violence.

Ben would have been fourteen years old when Jonesville planters burned their former slave houses, and well into adulthood when Manny Price, Robert Scruggs, and Jack Long were lynched. Myrtle Dudley, who provided an extensive record of her family life, recalled her father as a quiet man of stern moral standard, who would not allow cursing or drinking on his property, and thwarted corn thieves by putting traps in the walls of his corn crib.[29]

In 1877, Ben married Sara Frances "Fannie" Wynne, a woman of similar pioneer stock, who did not share her husband's quiet disposition. A Georgian by birth, Fannie was an older daughter of the enormous Wynne-Woodall family, one of thirteen children. Like many area planters, the Wynnes' roots were in South Carolina where they lived until shortly before the Civil War when they migrated to Georgia, eventually settling in Quitman, just above the Florida line.

In her letters, as well as her children's remembrances, Fannie Wynne Dudley emerges as a forthright woman with a hot temper and an iron will who once expressed a desire to "whip the old Nick" out of an erring brother-in-law. Her daughter Myrtle, who possessed a similar temperament, recalled Fannie as being strict with both her children and the family servants, the kind of woman who never had to ask for something twice.[30]

---

28   Ibid
29   Ben Pickard with Sally Morrison, *Dudley Farm, A History of Florida Farm Life*, Alachua Press, 2003
30   ibid

Under Ben and Fannie Dudley's stewardship, the Dudley holdings expanded and diversified to the point that it fulfilled Captain Dudley's vision of building an East Florida plantation. They survived the great freezes of 1897 that decimated local citrus farming, and steadily increased the size of their property holding to a peak of almost 900 acres. They emerged in the 20th century as a center of social life in the rough-hewn West End of Alachua County.

Larger in land mass than the county seat in Gainesville, the Community of Dudley, as it was sometimes called, sat at the crossroads of the Old Gainesville and Jonesville Roads in the prime location that Captain Dudley had hand-picked in 1858 when he was a road commissioner.[31] In the early 1880s, the original homestead dogtrot was abandoned (eventually it would house recalcitrant hogs) and a new board-and-batten main house was built that was more in keeping with Ben Dudley's status as a planter.

Figure 5. Dudley home and store, circa 1920. Courtesy of Florida Memory

---

31   Ben Pickard with Sally Morrison, *Dudley Farm, A History of Florida Farm Life*, Alachua Press, 2003

The imposing four-bedroom Georgian-style home was built with an eye to the Florida heat, with deep porches front and back, and a wide central hallway that offered natural ventilation. There was a piano in the sitting parlor that was large enough for entertaining company, and a steep central staircase that led to a large attic room which would eventually serve as a dormitory-style bedroom for Ben and Fannie's many children. The room faced south, with a large, double-window gable that looked out over the front yard, to the dirt crossroad of the Gainesville and Jonesville roads, marked by ancient fat cypress.

The heart of the home was twenty feet behind the main house in the two-room kitchen and dining room, which were built separately from the house for better insect control, and in fear of fire. The kitchen complex was well-equipped and large enough to be a world unto itself, which it was to the women, Black and white alike, who kept the fires lit and worked there from dawn until dusk.

The house and kitchen were the hub of the larger plantation, which was a model of self-sufficiency, with a two-loft barn, a tobacco curing shed, a smoke house, a grinding stone for sugar cane and corn, a dairy shed, an outdoor laundry facility, and a maze of fences and pens for livestock and poultry. The variety of buildings marked Dudley as a working plantation, which at the peak of its prosperity was second only to phosphate mining as the area's largest employer. Aside from truck farming, Dudley produced a variety of labor-intensive crops: tobacco, sugar cane, poultry, livestock, corn, fruit crops, and most profitably, thirty acres of Sea Island cotton.[32][33]

In the half-century since the Captain had first spied the property, the high rolling longleaf pine had been carved into fields and hedgerows, and planted with citrus, fig, and banana trees. Enormous

---

32   ibid
33   A successful cotton crop, pre-mechanization, required: plowing up the ground with plow and mule, planting the seed, hoeing the seedlings with a hand-held hoe, defoliating the plants by hand, picking the rough cotton bolls, and hauling the raw cotton by wagon to the Dutton gin in Gainesville. Prosperous, it was. Easy, it was not.

magnolia marked the western edge of the homestead, and fat old cypress marked the front gates, casting the yard in a deep, year-round shade.

Surface water was more available then, and there were two ponds on the property—one a certified swimming hole—and thirteen caves and shallow, fern-grown sinks. One was in a hammock on the crossroad, making it the perfect place for Cracker [34]cowmen to rest their cattle on a drive, with the blessing of Ben Dudley, who was known for his hospitality to travelers on the road.

Figure 6. Recreation of interior of Dudley store

The Dudleys ran a country store that sometimes acted as the farm commissary, from 1892 until 1916. The store was housed in a rough-boarded, windowless outbuilding that stood on the Gainesville Road, just west of the Dudley front yard. Ben's older daughters ran the store, which sold and bartered to neighbors and tenants all of

---

34   For more information on Florida Cracker cowmen, read *Cracker: Cracker Culture in Florida History*, Dana Ste. Claire, University of Florida Press, 2006.

the essentials of rural Florida life: seeds, feed and farm equipment, along with grits, sugar, coffee, tobacco, and that staple of country life, penny candy. A desk in the back served as the post office in the days before mail delivery, when picking up mail was a high point in any farmer's week.

The combination of post office and commissary made the Dudley crossroads a prime gathering spot for Jonesville farmers to visit and gossip while picking up their mail and weekly supplies.

Figure 7. Dudley Family. Courtesy Florida Memory Project

***

All but the oldest of Ben and Fannie Dudley's children were born on the family homestead. These included Dolly, Laura, Dora, Annie Virginia, Lelia, Edna, Winnie, Harvey, Ralph, Norman, and Frank. Myrtle was the baby of the family who would outlive her many siblings, leaving the farm and twenty-four surrounding acres to the State of Florida in 1992.

It is through Myrtle's eyes that we have an eyewitness glimpse of life at Dudley in the early part of the twentieth century, via two sessions of oral history taken with Lisa Heard and Sally Morrison in 1992, when Myrtle was ninety-one. The transcriptions of the recordings show Myrtle to be a forthright, family-proud woman who remembered grudges, kept score, and wasn't afraid to speak her mind. Though her financial status was fragile when she made the recordings, and the Dudley homestead so ramshackle that it was nearly uninhabitable, Myrtle's upbringing as the daughter of a socially prominent planter continued to inform her every word.

She did not bother to sugarcoat her childhood at Dudley, one of incessant labor in the face of what can only be described as Homeric challenge. In Myrtle's telling, the soft-spoken, put-upon Dudleys were an island of sanity in a sea of unfettered chaos. They were buffeted regularly by fit-throwing neighbors, thieves of every description, vindictive bulls, homicidal roosters, and a brace of sorry son-in-laws. Their hired labor was unreliable and dangerous, "two-legged animals," she called them. Nothing under the face of the sun, including nurse's training and marriage, was beyond caustic suspicion or outright dismissal. As Myrtle herself conceded, it made for "a hell of a life."[35]

Figure 8. Ralph, Harvey and Ben Dudley putting up hay. Courtesy of Florida Memory

35   Myrtle Dudley, Oral History Interview with Lisa Heard, February 25, 1992, pg. 44, Samuel Proctor Oral History Program Collection, P.K. Yonge Library of Florida History, University of Florida.

The Dudleys' perch at the top of the local food chain was occasionally challenged by their white neighbors (Mr. Griffin seemed an especial thorn in their flesh)[36] who groused about the family's preferential treatment in regards to the location of the school and post office. But in times of trouble, they all obeyed the hardbound rules of the Florida frontier, and were quick to support each other. According to Myrtle, "In this community, in the case of needing anybody in [a] death or anything like that, [we had a signal]. If they wanted just to notify you, they shot a gun once. If it got to where they thought they were going to have to have you, they shot twice. By the time they got that, the men got their horses saddled. When the third time came, they went right to them because it was an emergency."[37]

This bond of support between the Dudleys and their white neighbors did not extend to the Black farmers of Jonesville, as Myrtle made abundantly clear time and again, in her oral history. It makes for painful reading because Myrtle was, at age ninety-one, an entrenched and unashamed racist who rarely mentioned a Black tenant or servant by name, and instead relied on impersonal and disparaging invective.

To Myrtle, the Black labor that was essential to the operation of Dudley farm, who were paid in little more than bartered food and shelter, were the eternal, lowly "Other." Until her death, she never allowed a Black person, even a valued farm hand, into the Dudley house, aside from working domestics.[38] The closest she came to respect, not warm affection but at least acknowledgement of skill, was when she spoke of Becky Perkins who acted as "guardian" over Captain Dudley's wife and four children when the Captain was off to war.

---

36   Myrtle Dudley, Oral History Interview with Lisa Heard, February 25, 1992, pg. 15, Samuel Proctor Oral History Program Collection, P.K. Yonge Library of Florida History, University of Florida.
37   Myrtle Dudley, Oral History Interview with Lisa Heard, February 25, 1992, pg. 44, Samuel Proctor Oral History Program Collection, P.K. Yonge Library of Florida History, University of Florida.
38   Unnamed source, 2016

Perkins was Fannie Dudley's maid, nurse and family nanny who knew folk medicine and in fact saved Myrtle's life when she was born prematurely in 1901. "She was an ex-slave's daughter. That old nigger knew just what she was doing. They did not even dress me until in the spring. They had sheets up like that. I said it looked to me like they took a bed sheet and cut it up in two pieces and put me on it. They did not dress me until the spring of the year. They said there was not nothing there to dress."[39]

The hard racial language Myrtle used, even when allotting respect to a woman who'd saved her life, reflects not only the harsh prejudice of the day, but also what seems to have been a customary regard the Dudley family had for the Black workers who worked on their farm. It was a contempt common in in ex-slave holding families, especially ones who'd worked as overseers and slave-traders, as Captain Dudley had done.

In an interview with Ron Sachs that appeared in the *Gainesville Sun* in 1977, Myrtle's brother, Frank Dudley, used similar language, and equal contempt, when describing the 1916 lynching, with no fear of contradiction or alienating his audience.

According to Myrtle, the Dudley children had learned their racial manners at their mother's knee, noting that when Fannie Dudley regained consciousness after birthing Myrtle and found Becky Perkins' daughter nursing the premature Myrtle (thus saving her life), she "like to have had a fit," and "Trouble broke loose."

When questioned further about Fannie's rage, Myrtle stated plainly that Fannie was outraged because she "hated niggers the same as I do."[40]

Myrtle did not attribute her mother's hatred to the long shadow of the Civil War, or the racial violence that had raged across the

---

39   Myrtle Dudley, Oral History Interview with Lisa Heard, February 25, 1992, pg. 7, Samuel Proctor Oral History Program Collection, P.K. Yonge Library of Florida History, University of Florida.
40   ibid

South for most of her life, but to a more recent trauma—a Black man had killed her brother.[41]

That man was Boisy Long. Fannie Dudley's brother was Deputy George Wynne.

---

41   Myrtle specifically claims that two of Fannie's brothers were killed by Black men. She does not give the name of the other brother, nor the circumstances of his death.

Chapter Three

THE DEPUTY

Born in Alachua County in the chaotic days of Reconstruction in 1869, Samuel George Wynne, who went by the name George, was Fannie Dudley's younger brother. Both were children of a large, often-migrating family with roots in South Carolina who had most recently lived in South Georgia. Census records document the Wynne family moving back and forth between Quitman, Georgia and Alachua County several times in the late 1880s. They were living in Alachua County on the 1870 census when George Wynne was a baby and his sister Fannie ten years old. On the 1880 census, Fannie was married to Ben Dudley, living in Jonesville, while George Wynne and his parents and siblings were living in Quitman, a little more than an hour north.[42]

Wynne's mother died in 1882, and his father the same year by suicide. In a note on the Norris-Verbois family tree on Ancestry.com attached to Samuel George Wynne, Sr. says: "He was found dead in his bed. He was a heavy drinker. His wife had died several months earlier. He had made two failed attempts at suicide in as many years. He died from drinking chloral, a sedative." At age fourteen, Wynne

---

42   *Quitman Free Press*, August 20, 1916 reports that George Wynne grew up in Quitman. At some point, his family moved to Alachua County, but his ties to Quitman remained intact.

and his siblings were taken in to be raised by their sister Fannie, as was the custom of the day. George Wynne joined the work force at Dudley and when he was age thirty-three, homesteaded seventy-seven acres directly north of the Dudley homestead, in the vicinity of the original family dogtrot.[43] [44]

Four years later, on the 1900 census, Wynne was living with Ben and Fannie and eleven of the Dudley children, who considered their young uncle a beloved older brother. He could read and write, and his occupation was listed as farmer. Wynne was forty-one on the 1910 census. He lived with his brother Tom and Tom's wife and children on a farm adjacent to Dudley. Wynne was single, his occupation listed as deputy sheriff.

Wynne was appointed town constable of Newberry in 1909 after Marshall C. H. Slaughter was charged with embezzlement and removed from office.[45] He would hold both positions, as an Alachua County deputy and Newberry town constable until his death and was reelected as constable the last time in June, 1916.[46] As deputy, Wynne was one of fourteen who served under Sheriff P. G. Ramsey, then in his third term of office.

Wynne's official constable photograph, taken around 1907, shows a somber, handsome man, one with a future in higher law enforcement, possibly as the sheriff of Alachua County.

---

43   Ben Pickard with Sally Morrison, *Dudley Farm, A History of Florida Farm Life*, Alachua Press, 2003
44   Florida Homestead and Cash Entry Patents, pre-1908, document #12464
45   Though Slaughter lost his position in Newberry he was soon appointed Town Marshal of nearby Archer, where he served till 1912, when he and Deputy F. V. White were killed in a shoot-out with Cain and Fortune Perry, who were hung for the deed on September 30, 1912. (*The Miami Herald*, "State News Notes" September 30, 1912.)
46   *Gainesville Daily Sun*, "Former Marshall is Now in Trouble" May 20, 1909

Myrtle, who was fifteen when her Uncle George died, remembered him as a quiet and decisive man who was as well-loved in the larger community as he was within his family. "Everybody worshiped Uncle George. He was quiet with you. If he told you no, he meant no; if he told you yes, he meant yes."[47]

Figure 9. Samuel George Wynne, Florida Memory Project

Newspaper accounts written after Wynne's death, while universally complimentary, recalled a less-peaceable reputation. The local Gainesville paper said that George Wynne "bore the reputation as one of the most fearless officers in Alachua County."[48] The *Lakeland Evening Telegram* noted that Wynne had "many serious encounters with negros."[49]

The details of these encounters were not given, but Wynne was almost certainly present at the lynching of Manny Price and Robert Scruggs, where the mob poured bullets into the bodies after they were hanged. Local newspapers noted that deputies were in attendance, and had Wynne refused to participate, he would have lost the confidence of his constituents and his reputation for fierce enforcement, which was an essential requirement of lawmen of the day.[50]

---

47   Myrtle Dudley, Oral History Interview with Lisa Heard, February 25, 1992, pg. 8, Samuel Proctor Oral History Program Collection, P.K. Yonge Library of Florida History, University of Florida.
48   *Gainesville Daily Sun*, August 21, 1916
49   *The Lakeland Evening Telegram*, "Deputy Dies From Bullet Wounds." August 19, 1916
50   For further reading on the role of Sheriffs in Florida history, see *Florida Sheriffs: A History, 1821-1945*, William Warren Rogers, James M. Denham, (Sentry Press, 2001)

Fearlessness to the point of aggression was considered an especially necessary trait for the deputies of Beat Six, which covered one of the most lawless sections of the state. There were the saloons and bordellos of downtown Newberry as well as the Cummer lumber mill, a long stretch of the Atlantic Coastline Railroad, and the turpentine camp at Half-Moon. The railroad alone would keep a deputy on his toes, but Beat Six also included fourteen rough-and-tumble phosphate mines and a work camp that housed crews who were building the local section of the Dixie Highway.

All of these industries leased convicts who were doing time for crimes as small as vagrancy and as violent as murder. Perfectly described by historian Douglas Blackmon as "slavery by another name," convict leasing had become one of the answers to the severe labor shortage in the burgeoning economy of post-Reconstruction Florida. Convicts were rented from the state by companies who needed large labor supplies to do back-breaking work in phosphate mining, highway building, lumber harvesting and turpentine, then called naval stores.

The convict-work camps dotting the flat woods of the Big Bend area of Florida were isolated, primitive affairs—hot, brutal confines where underfed, overworked inmates were subject to whippings, tortuous confinement in the sweat box, and work under conditions as exploitative and abusive as slavery.[51]

The work camps on the West End of Alachua County were small, open-air penitentiaries, with the guards, the shotguns and bloodhounds on staff to chase fleeing convicts. The hounds were of such high quality that Deputy S. G. Livingston made a gift of two of them to Sheriff Ramsey in 1909 to use on county prisoners.[52]

---

51   An eyewitness account of life in early convict camps can be found in *The American Siberia, or Fourteen Years' Experience in a Southern Convict Camp,* by J. C. Powell (1891). See also Vivien Miller, *Hard Labor and Hard Time: Florida's Sunshine Prison and Chain Gangs.* (Gainesville: University Press of Florida, 2012).
52   *Gainesville Daily Sun,* "With An Ugly Knife Woman Slashed Man" September 16, 1909

That year the Gainesville paper reported, "The West End section, where practically all the phosphate mines are located, has been the scene of much disorderly and unlawful conduct, notwithstanding that the mine superintendents and officials have exercised every precaution to check them. This is due largely to the fact that many of the mines have worked convicts who are turned loose upon the community, with the result that they tarry in the vicinity, and trouble follows."[53]

Figure 10. Franklin Phosphate Company, Newberry, 1910. Courtesy of Florida Memory

Wynne's successful control of Beat Six, and the means he used to do it, often made headlines in the local papers in Gainesville. It was not uncommon for him—or any deputy of that day—to engage in gun battles, or fatally shoot suspects resisting arrest. The headlines

53   *Gainesville Daily Sun,* September 16, 1909

in 1909 alone include, "Deputy Wynne Gets Another Bad Negro"[54] and "Negro Murderer Caught by Wynne,"[55] "Deputy Sheriff Was Compelled to Kill."[56]

In September of 1909, a lengthy account of a roundup of suspects was reported in the *Gainesville Sun* under headline, "West End Section Was Very Lively; Promiscuous Raid of Negroes in Mining Section."[57] The raid was organized by Wynne and Deputy S. G. Livingston, who were "familiar with conditions in that section and in charge." The article reports "it was good game the officers captured," then goes on to list the suspects and their crimes (assault, killing a mule, and theft.)[58]

The use of hunting imagery as a metaphor for capturing, and sometimes killing, convicts was common in its day, as it was when describing the capture of lynching victims. Such imagery had two effects: it reduced the convicts to the status of wild animals, and it reassured citizens that their elected lawmen were doing satisfactory work rooting out the "bad Negros" and "Negro Desperados" across the West End.

Some deputies were more aggressive in dealing with Black suspects, and Wynne's reputation seems to put him on the harsh end of the scale. On May 13, 1912, Wynne was one of the first officers on the scene at the capture of a Black man from Archer named Cain Perry who was alleged to have murdered Constable Charles Slaughter and Deputy Charles White. Perry's arrest and subsequent trial have a bearing on the 1916 lynching, as it happened in neighboring Archer just four years earlier. Until Wynne's shooting, the double murder was the most notorious crime of the day.

Perry and his son Fortune were accused of decoying Constable

---

54   *Gainesville Daily Sun*, "Deputy Wynne Gets Another Bad Negro" September 24, 1909
55   *Gainesville Daily Sun*, "Negro Murderer Caught by Wynne" February 12, 1909
56   *Gainesville Daily Sun*, "Deputy Sheriff Was Compelled to Kill" March 01, 1909
57   *Gainesville Daily Sun*, "West End Section Was Very Lively; Promiscuous Raid of Negros in Mining Section." September 16, 1909
58   ibid

Slaughter—the same Charles Slaughter who had lost his job in Newberry several years before, for embezzling—to a rural house on a ruse that people were carrying illegal guns, and gambling. When Slaughter and two deputies—Charles White and J. A. Manning—approached the house, Cain and Fortune Perry opened fire, killing Deputy White and wounding Deputy Manning.

Manning feigned death and managed to escape, and Cain Perry, though wounded, also survived. According to the Tampa newspaper, Perry barricaded himself in his house and "threatened to kill anyone who tried to arrest him except Sheriff Ramsey, to whom he later surrendered."[59]

George Wynne was one of the deputies Perry specifically barricaded himself against, refusing to parlay, which indicates that the wounded Perry feared that any encounter with Wynne would cost him his life.

Sheriff Ramsey was able to persuade the wounded Cain Perry, along with three of his sons, to turn themselves in, and though there were threats of lynching, Ramsey was able to keep them safely in Gainesville. Of the six Black suspects arrested for Slaughter and White's murder, only Cain Perry, his son Fortune and Lige Brown stood trial. Brown was found guilty of a lesser count, but the Perry father and son were found guilty and sentenced to hang on the grounds of the Gainesville jail.

Racial tension ran high in the area, and on the eve of the Perry hanging, an anonymous letter, dated September 24, 1912, was sent to Archer Mayor C. W. Baldwin, that warned, "You better turn Cain and Fortune Perry loose, or we will burn the whole town. We told you we would burn Baulknight's store, and we did. We can kill more whites than you can negroes."[60]

Historian Lizzie PRB Jenkins believed that the letter came from

59 *The Tampa Tribune*, "Four More Negros Arrested for Assassination in Archer." May 14, 1912.
60 *Weekly Town Talk*, Alexandria, Louisiana, "Blacks Promise Arson If Negroes Are Hanged." September 28, 1912.

a group of prominent Black men from Archer, who were affiliated with the fraternal order Men of Worth, and called themselves "Night Riders."[61] [62]

Figure 11. Hanging of Cain and Fortune Perry, Gainesville.
Courtesy of Florida Memory

The threatening letter was reprinted in several papers, even nationally, and taken seriously by Sheriff Ramsey, who brought in

---

61   Lizzie PRB Jenkins, *Black America Series Alachua County Florida*, Arcadia Press
62   The Baulknight family were planters, who may well have owned a local commissary. There is no record that such a store was burned. If it was a plantation commissary, it might have been dealt with privately.

special police and increased night patrols in Archer.[63] There is no record of further threats, and Cain and Fortune Perry were hanged at the yard of the jail in Gainesville on September 30, 1912, in the same location where Boisy Long would be four years later.

Sheriff Ramsey presided, and both Perrys thanked him for his kindness, though neither died a particularly easy death: Cain Perry took nine and a half minutes to die, and his son Fortune strangled for a full ten and a half minutes.[64]

Public hangings were well attended by men, women and children, who sat on the nearby walls and climbed trees for a better view. The crowd at the Perry lynching was estimated as more than 2,000 spectators who came from not only Gainesville and Archer, but all the outlying towns including Newberry, the "bustling metropolis of the West End" three miles west of Dudley.[65]

---

63   *The Tampa Tribune*, "Archer People Will Repel Negro Attack." September 27, 1912.
64   *The Miami Herald*, untitled, September 30, 1912.
65   *Gainesville Daily Sun*, August 29, 1907.

Chapter Four

A REPUTATION FOR LAWLESSNESS

Figure 12. Downtown Newberry, 1907. Florida Memory Project

Turn-of-the-century Newberry was considered an upstart by its antebellum neighbors at Dudley, though it, too, was settled by South Carolinians in 1894 after the Savannah, Florida and Western Railroad (later bought by the Atlantic Coastline) was extended from High Springs through the town.

The Teague brothers from Newberry, South Carolina first named the Florida railroad station Newtown, and later Newberry, as if hoping the cut-over bit of wilderness would grow to emulate the gracious living they remembered in the long-established Carolina town. In the beginning, it seemed not an impossible plan, as Newberry was an up-and-comer in the area, a railroad town thirteen miles west of the county seat in Gainesville that was built on a bedrock of incalculably valuable hard-rock phosphate.

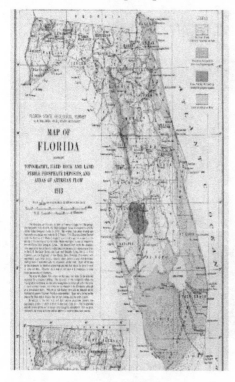

Originally discovered on the eastside of Alachua County by Dr. C. A. Simmons in 1880, phosphate was essential in the production of high-quality fertilizer. Mining it had burst into production on a large and profitable scale in 1889, in the Marion Phosphate Company, forty miles south in Dunnellon. Newberry's phosphate was coveted, and with close railroad access, it could be easily shipped, first to ports in Savannah, and eventually to Jacksonville.

Figure 13. Florida Phosphate Deposits, 1913.
Courtesy of Florida Memory

German industrialists invested in the mines, both as owners and buyers, as did the Cummer brothers in Jacksonville, who opened a phosphate and lumber operation east of town.[66] With the mines came a steady wave of prospectors, speculators, railroad

66   *Newberry The Early Years*, Don L. Davis.

men, and laborers, along with an attendant professional class of merchants, doctors, undertakers and preachers to support them.

Figure 14. Downtown Newberry, 1916. Courtesy of Florida Memory

The sudden inflow of money and miners created a town that was both literally and figuratively roughhewn. The high rolling pinelands of Western Alachua County had been largely cut over for its lumber, leaving Newberry to suffer from a grievous lack of shade, as noted by an unimpressed reporter from *The Crisis*[67] in 1916.

In time, with the new money from phosphate, the town assumed a more cultured exterior. A two-story Romanesque-style bank opened in 1913 one block west of the railroad, anchoring a sturdily middle-class community that contained an opera house, a theatre, several hotels, saloons, a high-end ladies' clothing store, an ice plant, a newspaper called *The Newberry Miner*, several physicians and three well-trafficked pharmacies.

---

67   *The Crisis* magazine is the official publication of the National Association for the Advancement of Colored People (NAACP) founded in 1910 by W. E. B. DuBois.

Figure 15. Suwannee Drug Company, 1920. Courtesy of Florida Memory

The city-owned light plant opened in 1916, providing one hour of electricity a night, and a two-cell, eight-bed jail was built next door, the iron doors repurposed from the lion cages of the circus train that delighted Newberry children when it passed through town on the way to the coast.[68]

The Gothic-Romanesque First Baptist Church, with stained-glass windows and a bell tower, opened in 1913, a block west of the bank and two blocks from the depot. The church, depot and bank anchored the downtown, which was soon surrounded by sturdy, high-ceilinged homes of the new professional class.

---

68   Katie Bea Cooke, 1993

Figure 16. Bank of Newberry, 1912. Courtesy of Florida Memory

A handful of the houses stand today, early-century Queen Anne, Craftsman and Cracker Vernacular styles, with deep porches and floors made of local heart pine so hard that it took a skilled carpenter to successfully drive in a nail by hand.

Figure 17. Getzen house, 1911. Courtesy of Florida Memory

For a brief few years, Newberrians achieved a life of genteel and artful ease. A puff piece about a social afternoon in a home in downtown Newberry that appeared in the *Tampa Tribune* in mid-August, 1916, a bare week before Deputy Wynne was shot, fairly drips with decorum: "The rooms for the occasion were decorated with potted plants and cut flowers. The guests were received in the drawing room by the hostess and honoree. After several games of cards, a salad course was served and later a delightful musical program was rendered."[69]

Figure 18. Newberry Depot. Florida Memory Project

Although the international nature of phosphate brought a steady stream of Northern businessmen, Midwestern salesmen and European prospectors to town, Southerners maintained a cultural majority, by far. Looking for a new start in Florida, many came from states that had been devastated by the war. They carried with them both the physical and psychological scars of war, and enforced Jim Crow as rigidly as if it had been handed down by Divine Law.

White supremacy was the working knowledge of the day in a

---

69   *Tampa Tribune*, "Newberry" August 13, 1916

town where minstrel shows were common entertainment, and segregation an accepted fact of life. Black Newberrians lived in the far northeast section of town in shacks[70] and shotgun homes—some owned, many rented. There were a few Black-owned stores in Newberry, and a few fortunate Black men secured better pay with the railroad. But most Black men in town worked in menial labor at the ice plant, saloons, and livery stables, while "many of the women go out to service to other cities."[71] The railroad the town had been built around ran north to south, cementing a racial division that would last into the next century.

Life under Jim Crow was severe, and Black Newberrians walked a thin line of correct behavior, with violence always a looming threat, as a local man named William Cowart boldly confessed in a letter he sent to the editor of *The Crisis*, dated April 1, 1911. *The Crisis* apparently had a readership in downtown Newberry, even among white people, as Cowart[72], a clerk at the Suwannee Drug Company, wrote an inflammatory letter to the editor concerning access to public libraries for Black patrons. Cowart was incensed at the very idea. With dripping contempt, he likened Black library patrons to animals, and openly confessed that, "The people of the South don't think any more of killing the Black fellows than you would think of killing a flea."[73]

The impassioned zeal in Cowart's letter reflected white Newberrians' disdain for any Black progress to the point of threatening murder, not in response to crime, but responding to the idea of Black citizens using the local library. The stringency of his

---

70   African-American historian Joel Buchanan, who had family in Jonesville, made a salient point in his oral history about the shacks of Alachua County: shacks were the only housing Black people were allowed to live in. Though primitive, they were proudly held, and in his experience, kept clean as a whistle.
71   *The Crisis*, October 1916.
72   Cowart was the stepbrother of William Barry, Sr. On the 1910 Federal Census for Newberry-Archer, Cowart was a drug salesman at the same pharmacy where Lem Harris was employed, the Suwannee Drug Store.
73   *The Crisis*, April 1, 1911.

fear might well have been connected to the fact that Blacks were the majority population on the West End by three to one, including the Black miners who moved earth with pick and hammer at the fourteen mines that surrounded the town. These Black men were not convicts, but instead were free Black men who were valuable workers in the state economy. Though legally compelled to abide by the indignities of Jim Crow, their dollar-a-day wages fueled the local economy.

The miners, Black and white alike, were a hardworking, hard-living crowd, and town constables like George Wynne were kept busy on Saturday nights when the miners came to town to spend their wages. Knifings, shootings and fatal bare-fisted fights were so common that the town supported the services of three full-time physicians. Old-timers described turn-of-the-century Newberry with head-shaking wonder because the rough-and-ready Newberry of illegal saloons and gambling dens lived side-by-side with socially-aspiring Newberry.[74] Two blocks from the bell tower of First Baptist were a pair of notorious bordellos, their existence so accepted that children of the era remember being in awe of the prostitutes and their lacy parasols when they were taken out in the afternoon for their daily carriage ride.[75]

The open saloons, prostitution and an abundance of gambling indicate that law enforcement in the area was of a flexible nature. The phosphate mines, Atlantic Coastline Railroad, and the convict camps all employed private security, many of whom went on to work in public law enforcement. These lawmen were required to be tough, and as a rule were, and it is worth noting that they themselves were frequently arrested, both in and out of office.

Their crimes ranged from embezzlement (Charles Slaughter) to murder— not just of fleeing suspects but, in the case of Alachua County deputy G. W. Livingston, cold-blooded double homicide. Livingston was Deputy George Wynne's closest colleague until

---

74   William Barry, Sr. 1993
75   Essie Neagle, 1993

November 1912 when he stood trial for a sensational double murder, in Brooksville Florida, of his former Newberry business partners, J. C. and Dave Long.

According to newspaper accounts, Livingston went to the Long brothers' sawmill in Brooksville to settle a dispute over six dogs. Witnesses at both the grand jury and the trial testified that Livingston approached the men, who were on horses, and told them to dismount, then shot them at close range with a double-barreled shotgun.[76] The first newspaper account noted "it is believed Livingston is demented and may try to take his own life."

Shortly afterward, carloads of Livingston's friends and supporters arrived from Gainesville and Jonesville, including W. J. Matthews, J. W. Miller, Deputy George Wynne, Sheriff P. J. Ramsey, J. L. and Glen Stringfellow, Thomas Kincaid, W. A. Strickland, T. E. Cellon, Larkin Carter, A. H. King and A. C. Reid. They were described as prominent, which wasn't hyperbole, as they were some of the wealthiest men in Gainesville. They shelled out $2,000 for Livingston's bond, then took him back to Newberry to await trial.

Livingston's friends from Alachua County helped him to find the best lawyers in Florida, and were in attendance in the packed courtroom when he stood trial on December 2. When the jury quickly found Livingston not guilty, there was so much cheering and hooting that Judge Bullock threatened to clear the chamber if they couldn't control their emotions.[77]

There is no record of a second trial, and Livingston returned to Newberry a free man, where he lived out his natural life as a building constructor, the husband of a woman active in the local Baptist Church. His acquittal on double murder charges, even with eyewitnesses' testimony and an abundance of motive, demonstrates the inequity of justice for white and Black Newberrians.

---

76   *The Tampa Tribune*, "Two Longs Killed Over Family Feud." November 6, 1912.
77   *The Tampa Tribune*, "Livingston is Found Not Guilty on Charge of Killing J. C. Long," December 1, 1902.

***

The roller-coaster ride of prosperity that built both sides of the Newberry tracks came to an abrupt end in 1914, when the assassination of an Austrian arch-duke touched off the powder keg of World War I. America was still isolationist at that point, but the German industrialists who bought Newberry's phosphate were blocked from doing business when shipping lanes in the Atlantic closed.

There was hope that the war would come to a quick end and mining would resume, but as the months passed into years, bankruptcy notices began to appear in local newspapers as merchants and businesses in Newberry were forced to shutter their doors.

By the summer of 1916, the inevitability of America entering the war, along with Newberry's continuing economic slide, made the dog days of August seem more sweltering than usual. An active hurricane season in the Caribbean had created a summer of storms, and boll weevil infestation was decimating local cotton farms, signaling the end of the guaranteed income that had kept many farms afloat. [78][79]

Added to the tension was an increasing labor shortage in naval stores, lumber, and highway building, as Northern companies lost their immigrant labor force due to the war, and began looking south for replacements. By 1916, Northern recruiters were openly meeting with Black workers in transportation centers like Jacksonville, promising them a better life in the big cities of the North, including thrice-better wages and freedom from the daily humiliation of Jim Crow.

Stress and uncertainty seemed to permeate every facet of life, including the political race between two men vying to be the Democratic Party nominee in the Florida Governor's race—a rabble-rousing preacher-turned-politician nativist named Sidney J. Catts,

---

78   *The Ocala Evening Star*, "The Summer of Storms" August 14, 1916
79   *The Tampa Tribune*, "Boll Weevil Cuts Cotton 20%" July 23, 1916

and his rival, the established, centrist William V. Knott. Newberry was a political town, with a resident State Senator, Daniel Gibbs Roland, and a mayor, Wallace Cleves, who owned the local newspaper, *The Newberry Miner*. The small town's political weight can be measured by the fact that Catts himself dropped by Newberry early in the summer on his famous barn-storming automobile-campaign tour and gave a rousing speech.

Figure 19 Sidney Catts campaign poster, 1916

Catts spoke extemporaneously in Newberry that June, and though no record of the speech remains, he almost certainly would have spoken at the picnic grounds off the Old Gainesville Road just east of town where summer political rallies were held—and lynchings, both popular public gatherings of the day.

The depth of Catts' involvement in the 1916 lynching in Newberry has yet to be thoroughly examined, though one of his race-baiting, pulpit-hammering speeches would have had an obvious effect on the events that followed that summer. He was running on a virulent anti-Catholic ticket, and was a proud white supremacist who wore two pistols strapped to his waist and openly admitted to having killed a Black man on his mother's plantation in Alabama.[80] Catts famously wooed rural whites, earning the famous quote by supporter Jerry Carter, that "The Florida Crackers have only three friends: God Almighty, Sears and Roebuck and Sidney J. Catts."[81]

---

80   Wayne Flynt, *Cracker Messiah, Governor Sidney J. Catts of Florida 1977*, pps. 86-87.
81   Ibid

Figure 20. Florida Governor Sidney J. Catts, 1917.

The race between Knotts and Catts was the talk of Newberry that summer, and indeed all of Florida, after Catts won the Democratic primary amid charges of lost-votes and ballot stuffing. So close was the count that Knotts challenged the vote, filling the local papers until the first week of August when the primary was momentarily displaced by a shocking crime in the nearby phosphate town of Kendrick.

At five p.m. on August 7, 1916, Constable Arthur Olin was shot by a Black phosphate miner named Albert Williams at the train depot. Olin had arrested Williams twenty minutes earlier for petty theft, but did not frisk him. While they sat at the depot waiting for the train to take Williams to jail in Ocala, Williams produced a high-caliber pistol and shot Olin three times, then fled. Olin was rushed to the hospital in Ocala where none of his wounds proved fatal, and Albert Williams was never apprehended for the deed.[82]

In a follow-up story, the Ocala newspaper made light of the shooting, quipping "it is hard to kill a good man. It is sometimes

---

82   *Ocala Evening Star*, "A Treacherous Act" August 7, 1916

hard to capture a bad one, for the negro who wounded Mr. Olin has not yet been captured."[83]

But this tongue-in-cheek banter, perhaps reflective of relief that Olin had survived with minor injury, was not in evidence in the county to the north, on the struggling West End of Alachua County. There, the loss of cotton to the boll weevil and a uncommonly rainy summer was proving as devastating an economic blow to local farmers as the loss of German trade had been to phosphate mining. Town and country people alike were having to count their pennies and tighten their belts, and among Jonesville farmers, a common complaint began to be murmured about missing hogs.

Always a staple in sustenance farming, hogs had lately gained value in North Florida after a market for them had opened in Georgia and in Jacksonville, where they could be shipped by train to processing plants. Hogs were not only prized for their meat, but for their quick growth—from piglet to market in six months. They were bringing a good price that year, being sold at ten cents a pound. So a farmer selling ten might make as much as $100 in profit, a huge return for the day.[84]

The problem with hog farming in Florida stemmed from the absence of fencing laws, which meant livestock could forage freely, without fences. Cows were branded and pigs identified by ear notches that were cut when they were piglets. The notches were registered with the county, and when it came time to gather these near-feral hogs for fattening, if the farmer's estimation of stock came up short, the possibility of theft was immediately raised.

Stealing hogs and changing notches was a serious crime—grand theft under Jim Crow—and punishable by up to five years of back-breaking labor in one of the local work camps. *The Crisis* reported that in Jonesville, "Many of the farmers have hogs which roam at

83   *Ocala Evening Star*, Untitled, August 15, 1916
84   *The Tampa Tribune*, "Etzler Some Hog Raiser" *September* 10, 1916

large in the road and in the woods. They are supposed to be branded but they are not always and there is constant trouble about them."[85]

There is no record of the official investigation into the missing hogs in Jonesville, no legal paper trail to explain if only one complainant was missing hogs, or if there was truly a neighborhood-wide problem with theft. All the farmers in the area, Black and white alike, kept unpenned hogs. The Dudley farm kept a hundred head that ran wild in the surrounding woods[86], and since there were no fences, precise numbers and accounting could not have been exact.

The little we know of the investigation isn't drawn from court records, but from three sources: newspaper accounts written immediately after the lynching; an article that appeared in October 1916 in *The Crisis*; and a piece of long-form journalism written in 1977 when Frank Dudley, the youngest son of Ben and Fannie Dudley, offered up the Dudley family's version of the events surrounding the 1916 Newberry lynching to a young investigative journalist named Ron Sachs.

Sachs interviewed Frank Dudley on his front porch near the then-dilapidated family farm. Dudley was seventy-seven and within three years of his death. Though he offered his account in the voice of an expert witness, his excessive smugness gives the tale the distinctive feel of a Cracker porch-yarn of a variety that is by definition something short of the gospel. He often contradicted the historic record, withheld details, and refused to name names, but his role as participant and first-hand witness sheds light in its own slanted way.

In this interview, Frank Dudley alleged that white Jonesville farmers were not only the victims of hog thieves, but of "an organized gang of thieves who'd steal anything that was left loose. It was the

---

85   *The Crisis*, "Another Lynching" *October 1916*
86   Ben Pickard with Sally Morrison, *Dudley Farm, A History of Florida Farm Life*, Alachua Press, 2003

biggest problem we had around here back then and the neighbors made up their minds that they were either going to run them niggers out or burn them out."[87] [88]

The time-line Frank Dudley set for this community-wide vigilante action is interesting, as it contradicted the voluminous newspaper accounts that followed the lynching in 1916. According to Dudley, the Dennis family had been *specifically* targeted by their white neighbors, who planned to "burn them out" long before Mills Dennis was arrested in Jacksonville, or Deputy Wynne attempted to serve any warrants. Note that legal action would not be used but instead, the same means would be employed that Jonesville planters had used against local freedmen fifty years before—the old terrorist tactic of burning them out.

We have no record of Deputy Wynne's level of participation in this vigilante plot, including whether his arrest of Mills Dennis was the first move in a larger action against the Dennis family, or if it was preemptive, to *avoid* it.

What we *do* know is that the first arrest connected to the investigation was of Boisy Long's adopted brother and cousin, eighteen-year-old Mills Dennis. He was arrested on Wednesday night, August 16, 1916 near Mayport, in Duval County. He was arrested by the sheriff himself, W. H. Dowling, on the charge of hog stealing.

Deputy Wynne went to Jacksonville the next day to bring Mills Dennis back to Gainesville. Most accounts agree that Wynne brought Mills Dennis to the Gainesville jail on the late train and then went on to Newberry, to look for two more men thought to be part of the gang."[89]

---

87   Ron Sachs, Sunday Magazine, "Conspiracy of Silence Shrouds 1916 Lynching," *Gainesville Sun*, November 7, 1977
88   Myrtle Dudley often presented herself and her family as victims of theft. Black tenants were accused of stealing cotton from the store, and corn. A white Gainesville physician was accused of land-theft and a nephew of stealing family heirlooms.
89   *The Lexington Progress*, August 25, 1916

The names of this "gang" were not given, but Mills Dennis' arrest brought Wynne into the home of a man who was well-known to Wynne, a man born on the J. J. Jones' farm across the road from Dudley, and who had almost surely picked up mail at the post office, and bought supplies at the Dudley Commissary.

That man was Boisy Long.

Chapter Five

THE ACCUSED

For more than a hundred years, the four men and two women who were lynched that weekend in Newberry in 1916 were nearly lost to history. The place of their deaths was remembered, if in abstract, but the victims themselves were little more than disembodied names, frequently misspelled, on an anonymous fatality roll.

The thoroughness of the century-long silence is complex. Foremost is the oath members of the mob took on the night of August 19, where they were made to touch the lynching rope to assure their complicity with the murders. So intimidating was the oath that the children and grandchildren of the mob, who grew up in Newberry, tell the same story of never hearing so much as a whisper about that night. If they walked in on a conversation where it was being discussed, the room would fall into immediate silence, with no questions acknowledged, answered, or allowed.

The descendants of the victims have also largely remained silent as well, refusing to discuss the lynching with people outside their community. James Dennis' children, who were present when he was taken by the hooting and hollering mob on the morning of August 18, were so profoundly traumatized that they feared for their personal safety if they spoke of it on the record, even eighty years later.[90]

---

90 Claudia Adrien, *Gainesville Sun*, "The Newberry Six" September 4, 2005

These families, who have lived in the same farming community for more than a century, have had to endure the lingering stigma of being labeled thieves, rogues, accomplices, and criminals. The accusations, never proven or tried in court, are part and parcel of the moral transgression that was put forth as excuse for the mob violence that shattered their lives. The descendants of the Dennis/ Long, and Young/McHenry families have denied the charges for a hundred years, to little effect as the disparagement is now cemented in the historic record.

In the absence of specific written or oral history, the lives of the Newberry lynching victims must be reconstructed by the slim historic records that remain: primarily the United States Federal Census and newspaper accounts of the day. The census is not foolproof, but is more reliable than the newspapers, as it is a standardized federal record not tainted by the echo-chamber that was created by the stringer reporters who descended on Newberry in the wake of the lynching. On deadline and in hot competition, these muckrakers tapped out stories that were conflicting, and when in agreement, were often cannibalized versions of previous reports. The supposed facts were anecdotal and often little more than hearsay.

The federal census from 1880, 1900 and 1910 all offer a sounder overview of the lives of James Dennis, Gilbert Dennis, Mary and Maria Dennis, Stella Young, Andrew McHenry, and J. J. Baskins, all Jonesville farmers living in multi-generational homes, and not thieves and scoundrels as portrayed by the white press.

The finer details of their lives before they were lynched were largely ignored, though *The Crisis*, which produced the only in-depth reporting, offers a glimpse of Black Jonesville in 1916. "Most of the land is under cultivation. Four or five large farms lie among the road, but most of them are small farms. Roads branch off from the main road leading to other farms. The chief products are cotton, corn, some sugar cane, peanuts, pecans, melons, cucumbers, and other garden truck. A large number of the farmers are Negroes. They own their own land, to a large extent, and are prosperous."[91]

**

One of the sons of these Black farming families was a young man named Boisy Long, who, like George Wynne, was an orphan— he'd lost his mother as a child, and was taken in to be raised by his extended family. So intertwined was Long's connection to the Dennis/Long and the Young/McHenry families that newspaper accounts variously described them as his cousins, in-laws and adopted family. They were, in varying degrees, all three.

Long himself was born in 1887 on J. J. Jones' plantation[92] just south of the Dudley homestead on the Jonesville Road. His orphaned status makes him difficult to trace on the census, as he sometimes went by other family names—Boisy Randolph, or Boisy Dennis. Family members say he was "taken in to be raised" by the Dennis family, who were his cousins."[93]

One of those cousins was James Dennis, who appeared on the 1910 census living in Jonesville with his wife, Julia. They owned their own property and after five years of marriage had three small children. The reporter for *The Crisis* described Boisy Long and James Dennis as neighbors, their houses "rather pleasantly located on a little rise of land on the (Gainesville) road, and are of the ordinary shanty type."[94]

James Dennis had deep roots in the Jonesville area. He was the son of Anthony Dennis and Jane Long Dennis, who had five children on the 1890 census. Though Anthony and Jane could not read, their children—James, Mary, Mills, Maria and Phillip—could.

91 *The Crisis*, "Another Lynching" October 1916
92 Unnamed source, Jonesville 2014
93 Claudia Adrien, "The Newberry Six" *Gainesville Sun*, September 4, 2005
94 *The Crisis*, "Another Lynching" October 1916

Anthony's mother, Maria Dennis, for whom her granddaughter was likely named, was born in South Carolina. She appeared on the 1870 census of Newberry with six offspring living in her household, and her occupation as a farm laborer.

Boisy Long and James Dennis were most likely cousins through the family of James's mother, Jane, who was born a Long, and married a Dennis. After Anthony Dennis' death in 1907, Jane married Allen Elliot. She and her new husband appeared in the 1910 census in a blended, multi-generational household, with two sons still living at home, and two daughters: Maria (whose name is sometimes transcribed as Mariah), and Mary.

In 1910, Maria and Mary were both widows with small children. They could read and write and were employed as farm labor. The patriarch of the Long family, Jane's father, Lewis Long, lived with them, at ninety years old. He was born in Georgia, and could read and write. James Dennis' older brother, Gilbert "Bert" Dennis, lived in nearby Archer, according to the 1910 census, with his wife and children. He was employed at a local lumber mill.

The census data indicates that the Dennis family was on an upward economic trajectory at the turn of the century. They were enslaved laborers in 1860, renters in 1900, and farm owners in 1910, with literate children who were steadily employed. Even the family's oldest member, Lewis Long, born in 1820, could read and write.

The descendants of the Dennis family have seldom spoken on the record about their extended family, and there are few alive today who can speak to the reputation of the family a full century after their deaths. One exception is the Reverend W. G. Mayberry, who is the grandson of Black Jonesville farmers. Reverend Mayberry grew up on stories told to him by his grandmother, who knew the Dennis, Long, McHenry and Young families well.

Mayberry was a featured speaker at a memorial for the lynching at Pleasant Plain Methodist in 2016, where he brought nostalgic laughter to the room reminiscing about life in the close-knit community that he described as poor, but aspiring, not above eating gopher and armadillo if that was the only meat to be had. Mayberry's grandmother knew the Dennis family and their adopted brother, Boisy Long. Mayberry paused a moment in his remembrance to find the perfect word to describe the Dennis family, and finally settled on "resolute."

The word seemed apropos, as the steady improvements the Dennis family made in education and home ownership, as noted on the census, in the face of vigilante violence and the stiff wind of Jim Crow, would have required nothing less.

THE YOUNG/MCHENRY FAMILY

The Young/McHenry family were also neighbors of Boisy Long on the 1910 census, living four households down from the Dudley homestead, making them very close neighbors indeed. Becky Perkins, who was a favored Dudley servant, was another neighbor, indicating that the Young and McHenry siblings were well acquainted with the Dudley family, though they owned their own land and were not Dudley tenants.

On the 1910 census, the head of the Young/McHenry family was a preacher, Reverend William Young, who was born in South Carolina in 1846, according to census. But his tombstone at Pleasant Plain says he was born in 1854. His wife, Della Stark, was born in Georgia and was a McHenry before she married William Young.

They had a blended family of seven children, five of them McHenry's: Malle, Andrew, Estella, Frank, and George. Andrew "Rew" McHenry worked for his stepfather on the home farm, as did his younger sister, Stella Young, who by 1916 was Boisy Long's wife and the mother of two of his children—toddler Randolph Murray and a female infant-in-arms.

The Young/McHenry family was doubtlessly one of the "prosperous Black farmers" of the Jonesville area *The Crisis* mentioned in its in-depth story. The article reported that the entire family could read and write and owned their own property. William Young's elderly grandmother, Jennie Childs, lived with them. She was born in South Carolina as were her parents, and though she could not read or write, her children and grandchildren could, an indication that the Young and McHenry family were, like their neighbors, building steadily improving lives.

THE BASKINS FAMILY

The Reverend J. J. (Joshua) Baskins was the oldest of the Newberry lynching victims, who was related to the McHenry's by marriage. He was born in 1871 in Jonesville, a younger son of Ruben and Eliza Baskins who were born in South Carolina. J. J. Baskins' family rented their house and were illiterate farm labor in 1880. By 1900, his siblings, who were still living in his parents' household, were presumably attending the Black primary school in Jonesville, or Liberty Hill school at Rutledge. As an adult, J. J. Baskins could read and write, and was both a farmer and a United Methodist preacher.

In 1910 he and his wife, Ellen, had been married thirteen years and had two daughters who attended school. The family rented their home, and all of them were employed as farmers. By 1916, according to *The Crisis*, J. J. Baskins "owned his own land, and was a preacher."[95]

***

These were the families of the Newberry lynching victims. Several of the men were preachers, and Jonesville was known to be a local center for Black Methodism. The rest were farmers or farm laborers whose extended family had worked in the Jonesville area their entire lives, as had their parents before them. Given that the Dudley Plantation was the largest employer in the area, it is reasonable to

---

95   *The Crisis*, "Another Lynching" October, 1916

assume that they not only knew the Dudley family, but had worked for them at some point and almost certainly had traded at the Dudley store where they would have picked up mail at the post office.

Whether there were thieves among them is impossible to judge from a hundred years' distance. The local newspapers do not record any imprisonment of members of the family in the years and months before the lynching, nor do any of the family names appear on the census of the local road camp, or phosphate mines in Dunnellon, where local prisoners were sent "off to the mines" to work out their sentences. The crimes they were accused of—aiding and abetting escape, and resisting arrest—were made *after* they were lynched, by the men who had murdered them, who, in the long light of history, do not seem nearly as reliable a witness as they were considered in their own day.

The fact that the Dennis family was already in the crosshairs of a vigilante action long before the night of August 18, is seldom mentioned in the larger history, though neighborhood feuds were far from infrequent on the Florida frontier.[96] The notorious Mizell-Barber feud in Orange County stretched out for years, and incited forty-one murders. The Whitehurst-Whidden-Stevenson feud in Pasco county, the Altman-Duncan feud in Baker County, and the Towles-Brannen feud in Taylor County were also drawn-out grudge-matches. Most were incited by accusations of livestock or land theft, though the Langford-West feud in Madison was provoked when a Langford insulted one of the West men's mother. All ended in multiple retaliatory murders. The frontier code of honor, which called for revenge in the case of shed blood, fueled the fires of vengeance and might well have played a part in the Newberry affair.

In her oral history, Myrtle Dudley does not go into great detail, but does say that her brother Harvey Dudley, the oldest son of Ben and Fannie Dudley, carried a grudge against a local Black preacher. She does not relate the nature of the grudge that was so bitter that

---

96   Elias Sapp's shooting in 1908 by Jack Long was part of a larger feud between the Sapps and the Longs.

Ben made Harvey accompany his mother to Jacksonville when his Uncle George was shot, to keep him out of the Newberry fray. "He [Ben] stayed here and let Mother go with Harvey. I am glad she carried Harvey, because there was a special nigger they [the mob] did not get that Harvey would have got."[97]

Myrtle insisted that Harvey's hatred wasn't directed at J. J. Baskins, but instead at *another* Black preacher, someone the mob did not lynch. The identity of this preacher is intriguing and difficult to determine, as several Black preachers lived on the verge of the Dudley plantation and had ties to the larger history. William Young, the father of Stella Young and Andrew McHenry, is listed as a reverend on the 1910 census, as was Squire Long.

Myrtle's strategic dissembling allowed her to speak of the matter without pinning anything on her brother Harvey, whom she described as being, in 1916, "a big strapping boy."[98] He was, in fact, age twenty-four at the time of the lynching and would have been long accounted a man. Myrtle's hints of a feud leave an intriguing and likely unsolvable mystery, one that makes a salient point; *there is much we do not know.*

What we *do* know is that the basic narrative of the Newberry lynching—that a random white deputy was shot while serving a warrant on a random hog thief—is a simplistic, streamlined summary that ignores a far deeper history. That history included a complex and on-going tribal war drawn along racial and caste lines on the West End of the county that had erupted into violence many times before, both legally and in vigilante action. It absolutely informed the actions of the two men who faced each other in the vacant tenant shack in the early morning hours of August 18, 1916, high-caliber pistols in hand.

The results were tragic. In the context of their broader history, it is hard to imagine it otherwise.

---

97   Myrtle Dudley, Oral History Interview with Lisa Heard, February 25, 1992, pg. 40, Samuel Proctor Oral History Program Collection, P.K. Yonge Library of Florida History, University of Florida.
98   ibid

Chapter Six

VACANT SHACK ON THE OUTSKIRTS OF TOWN

Figure 21. Farm house, Newberry. Courtesy of Florida Memory

Sometime after Mills Dennis' arrest on Thursday afternoon, Deputy Wynne delivered him to the Gainesville jail on the late train, then traveled on to Newberry, acting on a tip that two members of the hog-stealing gang were holed up on the outskirts of Newberry. The description of the house varied. *The Crisis* described it as "the usual shack variety" next door to Boisy's cousin James Dennis, on the Old Gainesville Road.

Most accounts agree that Boisy was asleep in his bed when Deputy Wynne knocked on his door at two in the morning. Wynne was accompanied by two white Newberrians in their twenties, neither of whom was a sworn deputy—Grady H. Blount and Lemuel G. Harris.[99] [100]

G. H. Blount was a Georgia-born newcomer to the area who had worked his way up from mule-driver to overseer at a local lumber camp. He was married to a Newberry schoolteacher and was an early automobile enthusiast who would eventually open one of Newberry's first gas stations. In 1916, Blount made extra income hiring out as a driver of a new eight-cylinder car he owned, of which he was very proud.[101] Since Deputy Wynne did not own a car, it is reasonable to assume that Blount was brought along in his capacity as driver, as he waited outside Boisy's home while Deputy Wynne entered with Lem Harris to make the arrest.

Lemuel "Lem" Harris was a native of Columbia County, and he also owned a car. He worked at the Suwannee Drug Company for the Barry family, and was referred to in the local social pages as the "popular young pharmacist in Newberry." Harris was also married to a schoolteacher; they had two small sons in 1916, one an infant.[102]

---

99   According to L. G. Harris' family, he was younger than his census record reflects. He changed his date of birth in order to enroll in pharmacy school, making him barely out of his teens in 1916.
100   *Lakeland Evening Telegram,* August 19, 1916
101   *Tampa Tribune,* "Newberry" August 13, 1916
102   Ibid

Figure 22. Drs. Getzen and Ruff, and Lem Harris, 1911. Florida Memory Project

Harris would survive the wounds he suffered in the shootout with Boisy Long, and moved to Clearwater in 1928. According to his great-granddaughter,[103] his descendants rarely, if ever, spoke of the shooting in Newberry, and had no clue why Harris accompanied Deputy Wynne in Long's arrest. *The Crisis* reported that there were rumors that Harris owned the stolen hogs,[104] which is possible, though Harris and his wife had just built a new house in downtown Newberry on the same street as Dr. Getzen, and had no farm property in Jonesville. Why a young pharmacist would be deputized in the middle of the night to help arrest a man later described as being "possessed of a mean disposition"[105] is difficult to say, and remains one of the small mysteries that surround that night.

Another unanswered question is whether Stella Young and her children were home when her husband was arrested, and if she, or any of her family, witnessed the gun battle. *The Crisis* admits that

103   M. Harris, 2018
104   *The Crisis,* "Cowardice" October 1916
105   William Wilbanks, *Forgotten Heroes: Police Officers Killed in Early Florida, 1840-1925,* 1998

the author "does not know if Stella Young was at the house at the time of the shooting."

There is also the issue of why Deputy Wynne served the warrant at two in the morning. In the furiously penned article that appeared in *The Crisis*, the timing of the arrest was called out as improper. "[A]n extraordinary thing to do—to go out on a lonely road to arrest a man at this hour."[106]

To Deputy Wynne, the timing of the arrest might not have seemed so extraordinary, as the lonely roads between Newberry and Jonesville were well known to him, being almost literally his own backyard. The timing was most likely chosen because Wynne was a strategic thinker when it came to apprehending suspects. He wanted to arrest the suspected members of the hog-thieving ring when they were unarmed and therefore less capable of resistance, having just wakened from sleep.

At trial,[107] both the state, and Boisy Long agreed that Long was in bed asleep when Wynne and Harris knocked at his door, woke him, and told him to dress. Wynne did not search Long for a weapon because he had just awakened him from sleep, and while Long got dressed, Wynne checked his bedcovers for a weapon, with Lem Harris covering both of them, pistol in hand.

According to the state's case, while Wynne was searching his bedding, Long drew a pistol he had strapped to his waist and shot him, two shots in "rapid succession"[108] at close range. When Lem

---

106   *The Crisis,* "Another Lynching" October 1916

107   Quotes taken from the trial transcript are sourced from William Wilbanks' *Forgotten Heroes: Police Officers Killed in Early Florida, 1840-1925* which was published in 1998. Wilbanks quotes from the trial transcript, though a records request made to the Alachua County Courthouse in 2019 yielded no record, other than two pages of handwritten notes from the Special Term of the Court on September 7, 1916, which includes the names of the jury, along with the charges and verdict. Lem Harris, Grady Blount and Tom Wynne are all listed as witnesses, though the record of Harris' testimony in the trial transcript itself is unknown; a grievous loss, as Harris was an eyewitness.

108   *Quitman Free Press,* August 20, 1916

Harris tried to wrestle the gun from Long, Long shot Harris in the shoulder and twice in the hands.[109]

Wynne and Long exchanged fire a second time, with Wynne hit four times, one a defensive wound to the wrist, the other three to his body. Wynne returned fire and hit Boisy Long in the arm as he ran to the door, making him stumble before he regained his footing and disappeared into the night in his bedclothes.[110]

**

Boisy Long's testimony of the evening, given under oath at his trial the following October in Gainesville, before Judge J. T. Willis and a jury of seven white men, differed in a few details. He agreed that Wynne woke him from sleep and told him to get dressed. Long testified that his pistol lay on his shirt on a chair behind the door. He had to pick up the pistol to get to his shirt, and when Wynne caught the movement, he thought he was pulling on him, and shot him. Long returned fire, or in his own words "went to shooting both ways and run."[111]

At trial, the doctor who treated Wynne in Jacksonville testified to the location of his wounds: four of them, to his liver, wrist and lungs; the first two considered fatal.[112]

Boisy Long's body was not autopsied after his execution in October, and if his wounds were ever treated by a doctor there is no record of their location. One newspaper account says he was shot in the arm, though the exact placement of the wound wasn't mentioned. A front entrance wound would support his testimony of Wynne shooting first. A back entrance wound would support the

---

109   The Quitman newspaper said Long shot the gun from Harris' hands.
110   William Wilbanks, *Forgotten Heroes: Police Officers Killed in Early Florida, 1840-1925*, 1998
111   ibid
112   ibid

state's case that Wynne was on the floor when he shot Long who was attempting to escape.

Grady Blount took the stand and gave an ear-witness account of the night, as he didn't go inside, but was waiting in his car when he heard six shots in rapid succession. He ran inside and found Harris and Wynne "writhing in blood." According to Blount, Deputy Wynne said he was going to die and that they must save Harris.[113]

Blount loaded Wynne and Harris into his car and drove them three miles west to Drs. Getzen and Weeks in downtown Newberry. Their arrival must have caused a dreaded commotion in the neighborhood in the still-dark hours, with baying dogs, lighting lanterns, and phoning Sheriff Ramsey.

Newberry doctors were accustomed to being wakened in the night to make quick assessments and treat traumatic wounds. Harris had lost a lot of blood, but the wounds to his hands and shoulder were treatable. George Wynne's abdominal wounds were far more grievous, so extensive that the local doctors deemed them fatal.

According to Myrtle Dudley, Wynne was conscious and knew that he was mortally wounded. He asked ("begged" in Myrtle's estimation) to be taken to his sister's house at Dudley farm to die, but someone in high authority, whom Myrtle refers to as "the state man,"[114] insisted on sending him to the Roger's Sanitarium in Jacksonville for a last-ditch emergency operation that might save his life.[115]

Several accounts say that Wynne was taken by train to Jacksonville, but Katie Bea Weeks Cooke, who was age six and in the neighborhood at that time, said that her uncle, William H. Tucker, drove Deputy Wynne to the depot in Waldo in his Model-T Ford.

---

113   ibid
114   Myrtle Dudley, Oral History Interview with Lisa Heard, February 25, 1992, pg. 9, Samuel Proctor Oral History Program Collection, P.K. Yonge Library of Florida History, University of Florida.
115   *Lakeland Evening Telegram*, "Five Negroes Killed Today in Newberry in Battle with Whites," August 19, 1916

Tucker was making for the depot in Gainesville, where Wynne could be placed on the Jacksonville train. Barely conscious, Deputy Wynne rose up in the back seat and reminded Tucker that the western gate of the University of Florida was locked at ten at night. Wynne's last words were, "The gates will be locked," before he lost consciousness and fell back in the seat.

Tucker avoided the locked gate by taking Wynne to the depot in Waldo, where the Atlantic Coastline held the train for him for an hour, to no effect, as Wynne died en route to Jacksonville.

Figure 22. Gates of University of Florida, 1910. Courtesy of Florida Memory

From Myrtle we have a first-hand account of the Dudley family's reaction to the news of the shooting of their Uncle George, which would have come to them sometime in the pre-dawn hours of August 18, to their front door at Dudley.

Myrtle recalled, "We kids all ran out to see what was the matter. Mother went to crying so when they told her how Uncle George was shot."[116]

---

116   Myrtle Dudley, Oral History Interview with Lisa Heard, February 25, 1992, pg. 10, Samuel Proctor Oral History Program Collection, P.K. Yonge Library of Florida History, University of Florida.

Fannie left immediately and took Harvey along to keep him out of the brewing trouble. According to Myrtle, "They got him [George Wynne] back to here, and then they got him on to Newberry and caught the train up here on the other side of Alachua and held it until they could get him and carry him to Jacksonville. But he was dead when they got him to Jacksonville. Mother said that if she had seen him before he left up yonder, she would not have let them carry him."[117]

Fannie Wynne Dudley wanted to bring her brother's body back to Jonesville for burial, but was overruled, possibly by Sheriff Dowling, who would have been the decision-maker in Jacksonville. By then, one man had been killed and an entire family taken into custody. It was clear that a race war was brewing in Newberry, and authorities in Jacksonville judged a funeral in Jonesville would be too incendiary.

In consequence, George Wynne never returned to his home in Florida but was buried at eleven next morning at the Old Cemetery in Quitman, Georgia, in the Wynne family plot, next to his mother, as requested, with "Mr. and Mrs. T. W. Wynne, Mr. and Mrs. M. T. Wynne, Mrs. P. B. H. Dudley, and P. H. B. Dudley Jr."[118] in attendance. George Wynne was forty-seven.

---

117   Myrtle Dudley, Oral History Interview with Lisa Heard, February 25, 1992, pg. 8, Samuel Proctor Oral History Program Collection, P.K. Yonge Library of Florida History, University of Florida.
118   *Quitman Free Press,* untitled, August 20, 1916

Figure 23. Samuel George Wynne's Woodman of the World tombstone,
Quitman, Georgia.

Chapter Seven

ALL THE COUNTRY UP IN ARMS

While Henry Tucker raced to get Deputy Wynne to the train in Waldo, a fury took hold of the West End of Alachua County that was uncommon even by Newberry standards, as word spread of the shooting. Sheriff Ramsey immediately formed a posse on horseback that, according to Frank Dudley, was armed with "shotguns, rifles, pistols."[119]

Albert Williams' escape in Kendrick two weeks earlier was, no doubt, on the sheriff's mind as he immediately set out to track the trail of the wounded Boisy Long. Lyman Long, a Black neighbor of the Dennis family, who was a small child in 1916, remembered seeing the men on white horses accompanying the sheriff, who came to question Lyman's father about Boisy Long.[120]

While Sheriff Ramsey carried on an official investigation, white Jonesville farmers began to gather on their own. Frank Dudley reported that "White neighbors went around to every nigger house and told them to stay inside that night. That was a point made especially strong to the niggers in that Dennis home."[121]

---

119   Ron Sachs, Sunday Magazine, "Conspiracy of Silence Shrouds 1916 Lynching," *Gainesville Sun*, November 7, 1977
120   Claudia Adrien, *Gainesville Sun*, "The Newberry Six," September 4, 2005
121   Ron Sachs, Sunday Magazine, "Conspiracy of Silence Shrouds 1916 Lynching," *Gainesville Sun*, November 7, 1977

Later in the morning, after full light, another element entered the expanding mob—a group of particularly inflamed men in automobiles who were described as George Wynne's "closest friends."

The Jacksonville paper reported that "on news of [Wynne's] death, more than a score of automobile loads of white men went from Gainesville to search for his murderer."[122] If the reporter wasn't exaggerating, that would mean twenty automobiles, speeding west on the craggy, washed-out limestone of the Old Gainesville Road, not under the supervision of Sheriff Ramsey but following their own agenda, intent on personal revenge.

James Dennis, Boisy Long's neighbor and cousin, was their first victim. Newspapers would later report that Dennis was killed while resisting arrest, but Frank Dudley, from the comfort of his front porch sixty years later, recalled it differently.

He said that while the sheriff's posse was searching, neighbors of the Dennis family warned them to stay inside. Hours later, when the men in the automobiles showed up, they found James Dennis outside of his house. When he "could not explain his presence," he was shot twice in the back with a shotgun. Another mob member turned Dennis' body over and shot him in the face with a .38 pistol.[123]

Frank Dudley identified one of the shooters as a neighbor, and several news accounts point to a deputy, while at least one account points to Sheriff Ramsey himself.[124] Landis Ross, the son of Black Jonesville farmer Albert Ross, who was a teenager in 1916, had a different account of James Dennis' murder. Ross said the men in the automobiles didn't arrest or serve a warrant on James Dennis, but abducted him for interrogation.

The place of interrogation was within earshot of Dennis' home—close to Dudley plantation, if not *at* Dudley—where they ordered James Dennis out of the car and to open the gate. When he did so,

122   *The Florida-Times Union*, August 19, 1916
123   ibid
124   *Pensacola News Journal*, August 20, 1916

one of them shot him in the back with a double-barreled shotgun, and another turned him over with his foot, and pumped two rounds into his face at close range, striking him so violently that pieces of his skull were embedded in a nearby post.[125]

Frank Dudley's account made light of James Dennis' murder, retelling it in a cavalier way that did not name names, or expose the exact location where the mob took James Dennis before killing him. He also neglects to mention that James Dennis was a family man who had committed no crime, who was taken from his home in the presence of his terrified wife and young children, all helpless to stop the hooting and hollering mob.

When Julia Dennis and her children next saw him, he had been shot beyond recognition, a sight so grievous that James Dennis' children trembled when they remembered it in old age.[126]

Local newspapers reported that Dennis was shot while resisting arrest, a distortion of the truth so galling to his family that when his widow read the lie in 1916, she resolved to never read another newspaper, an oath she followed until her death, in 1974.[127]

***

In the hours after James Dennis' murder, other members of Boisy Long's family were taken into custody: Mary, a heavily pregnant Maria Dennis, Long's wife, Stella Young, and her half-brother Andrew "Rew" McHenry. They were later accused of a slate of differing crimes, from stealing hogs to resisting arrest, to aiding and abetting a fleeing felon. The Jacksonville paper was more specific, and probably the most accurate. It reported that all were taken because they "resisted efforts of the posse to gain information."[128]

Sometime that day, James Dennis' older brother Gilbert "Bert"

---

125   *A History of Florida Through Black Eyes,* Marvin Dunn, 2014
126   Patricia Hilliard-Nunn, 2014
127   Ibid
128   *The Florida-Times Union,* August 19, 1916

Dennis (he is listed on the state record as "Burke" Dennis) who lived in Archer and worked for a sawmill, was arrested—or simply abducted—when he went into Newberry to buy his brother a coffin.[129]

The details of the custody of all of the Newberry lynching victims is not clear in the record. Most newspaper accounts reported that the Dennis and McHenry siblings were taken to the Newberry jail and held there, as was J. J. Baskins, though Frank Dudley was curiously insistent that they were not.[130]

Frank doesn't say where they were held, though Myrtle says that the Dudley property was where the men went, where the "action was." Some of the action happened within sight distance of the Dudley house, possibly at the Dudley store, which then fronted the Gainesville Road, and was a community meeting place. The Dudley daughters, who were locked up in the house, had crept upstairs to peep out of the upstairs window, which had a better view of the commissary, a few hundred yards to the west.

Certainly, the men were close enough to the house for Myrtle Dudley to report on them. A firsthand witness, a white man, saw members of the family weaving the lynching ropes at the kitchen table.[131] Myrtle was close enough to the mob to describe them in detail. Even she, who seldom lacked for words when describing grievance, found it hard to adequately depict an incandescent rage so physically transforming that it made those in the posse nearly unrecognizable.

"They were in such a tantrum and I do not know what all you would call it. But they did not look natural."[132]

Reverend J. J. Baskins was an outlier among the lynching victims. He was twenty years older than the others and not related to Boisy

129   *The Crisis*, "Another Lynching," October, 1916
130   Ron Sachs, Sunday Magazine, "Conspiracy of Silence Shrouds 1916 Lynching," *Gainesville Sun*, November 7, 1977
131   Patricia Hilliard-Nunn, 2014
132   Myrtle Dudley, Oral History Interview with Lisa Heard, February 25, 1992, pg. 9, Samuel Proctor Oral History Program Collection, P.K. Yonge Library of Florida History, University of Florida.

Long by blood. Yet, he was taken from his wagon as he returned to his farm from the market in Newberry. Most newspaper accounts, and hence, most histories, say he was held at the jail with the others and lynched at the same time, though both *The Crisis*, and Frank Dudley said that Baskins was not taken to the jail, but immediately hung "at a group of trees near Newberry"[133] presumably at the old picnic grounds, described as "a lovely little grove."

Throughout the Reverend Baskins' abduction and arrest he was said to have prayed aloud for the life of his wife, and to have called out to God to reveal his innocence to the mob. At least one prayer was answered—his wife Ellen was not killed.

Myrtle Dudley insists that Baskins was *not* the Black preacher who had incurred Harvey Dudley's wrath, though Baskins' death did warrant a specific, personalized violence that the other victims did not endure: Oral history in the Black community in Jonesville says that when Baskins' corpse was cut down, a member of the mob cut a long section of skin from Baskins' back that he planned to cure and weave into the tip of a "cracker whip." The man who took this grisly souvenir was said to be a doctor. [134]

News of Reverend Baskins' murder did not immediately reach his congregation, and on Sunday morning, a day after his death, the group gathered in the pews at his church for their regular morning service, as yet unaware that their minister had been lynched.[135]

Most lynching victims sank into the hard ground of history without a trace, but even in the poverty and violence of 1916, Reverend Baskins' family took care to memorialize him with an epitaph of uncommon tenderness that stands in stark contrast to the cruelty of his death, and desecration of his corpse. The aged and cracked tombstone still stands beneath the oaks at Pleasant Plains with an inscription so worn it is nearly illegible, that reads with sweet simplicity:

---

133 *The Crisis*, "Another Lynching," October, 1916
134 Patricia Hilliard-Nunn, memorial service at Pleasant Plain Methodist Church, August 2019
135 ibid

Rev. J. J. Baskins
Born 1871
DIED
Aug 18 1916

Kind father of
love thou art
*gone to thy res*t

Figure 24. J. J. Baskins tombstone, Pleasant Plain

***

As news of James Dennis' murder spread, the Black community on the West End fled east to Gainesville by foot, horse and wagon, intent on evading the armed white men who continued to pour into Jonesville. Some whites came out of curiosity, some to be part of the hunt. They were armed and dangerous, but were not associated with the men in automobiles who'd abducted and murdered James Dennis and were still wreaking havoc on the Old Gainesville Road.

Meanwhile, the official posse continued to search not only for Boisy Long, but for anyone connected to him by blood or marriage who might have knowledge of his whereabouts. To escape them, Long's nine-year-old son was said to have hidden in the hammocks of San Felasco, possibly the Warren Cave, six miles northeast of Jonesville toward Rutledge.

Mary Dennis and Stella Young were accused in the press of providing food or clothing to Boisy Long, but he testified at his trial that he had no assistance in his escape. The Gainesville papers had reported on Saturday that "Long is supposed to have stayed in hiding throughout the day in Denton hammock, five miles west of this city." There were other sightings of him in Arredondo, an area so vast that several sections of Alachua County went by the name. The shipping station of Arredondo was southwest of Gainesville, neighboring the Haile Plantation. The area called Arredondo where Boisy Long was said to have hidden was northwest of Jonesville, and there were other sightings along the Jonesville/Gainesville divide near the Stringfellow plantation.[136]

***

While the growing mob searched for Long, at least four members of his family—siblings, cousins and a sister-in-law—were held captive for fifteen hours between mid-morning on Friday and two early Saturday morning.

---

136   *The Tampa Tribune*, August 20, 1916

Wherever they were held—at Dudley, or in Newberry, at the small jail adjacent to the electric plant—the interrogation of Mary and Maria Dennis, Stella Young, Gilbert Dennis and Andrew McHenry was undoubtedly an emotional and terrifying ordeal. Maria Dennis was heavily pregnant[137] and according to *The Crisis* "it is said that the two women were tortured for information."[138]

Frank Dudley admitted to the beating of Maria Dennis, which he minimalized to "taking a strap to her bottom."[139] He said she was then set free and told to leave town in consideration of her unborn child, an admission the Black community of Newberry and Jonesville frankly doubt. It is more commonly believed that Maria didn't leave town at all, but was among the murdered.

In Jonesville, there are stories of her being dragged by one of the automobiles; stories have been related in the community for a hundred years, with no evidence to support or deny, as both she and her baby disappeared from the census afterward, which indicates that she either didn't survive, or changed her name, as many survivors of racial violence did.[140]

***

One of the few first-hand accounts of the lost hours on Friday are courtesy of Myrtle Dudley, who offered a unique snapshot of the day from ground zero, at the Dudley homestead, beginning in the pre-dawn hours when news arrived that her Uncle George had been shot.

Myrtle remembered that her mother, Fannie, "went to crying," and that her father, Ben, was the soul of practicality. Ben told Harvey to go with his mother to Jacksonville, and he put one of his older

---

137   Stella Young had an infant in arms and a toddler at home. According to Frank Dudley, Maria Dennis was pregnant. Ron Sachs, Sunday Magazine, "Conspiracy of Silence Shrouds 1916 Lynching," *Gainesville Sun*, November 7, 1977
138   *The Crisis*, "Another Lynching," October, 1916
139   Ron Sachs, Sunday Magazine, "Conspiracy of Silence Shrouds 1916 Lynching," *Gainesville Sun*, November 7, 1977
140   Patricia Hilliard-Nunn, 2014

daughters[141] in charge of her sisters. Ben told the older daughter to keep the other sisters in the house, on the first floor, even if she had to switch them.[142]

Figure 25: Girls' bedroom and stairway Dudley homestead

"He told us to get in the house and stay there, and we done it. We would go upstairs a time or two and peep out. If he heard us up there, he would tell us to get downstairs where we belonged. But he said he thought he would be better with all the girls. All of the eight girls were here. He sent Frank, my brother, on a horse or mule the next morning to tell Aunt Nerva.[143] When he got to the other end of

---

141   Myrtle says Laura was the sister put in charge, but Laura Dudley had died of appendicitis in 1914. More likely, it was Mary Dudley McLarty or Dora Dudley Pickett.

142   Myrtle Dudley, Oral History Interview with Lisa Heard, February 25, 1992, pg. 10, Samuel Proctor Oral History Program Collection, P.K. Yonge Library of Florida History, University of Florida.

143   Minerva Wynne Wright McQueen, who lived four miles northwest of Dudley in the Forest Grove community

this lane, [there were] four dead niggers piled up in a pile. He like to have went to pieces."[144]

Myrtle's memory of the day, like all of her memories in connection with the lynching, was selective and self-serving, but more emotionally honest than the almost jaunty picture her brother Frank painted. Frank Dudley made no mention of "going to pieces" at the sight of the corpses.

Myrtle recalled a day of great tension and grief, of being shut up with her sisters in a hot house in August, surrounded by the rage of a mob, and so frantically curious that they occasionally defied their father to run upstairs to squint out the higher windows for a closer look.

There is no record of what they saw, though Myrtle does put at least some of the action at Dudley, where men wanting to join the mob would "come here and want to know where the men were at, whether they went that way or whether they went this way or which way they went. They wanted to go where the crowd was."[145]

Like all racial constructs, the lines drawn at Dudley that weekend were far more complicated than simple Black and white. Even as the murderous mob combed the backwoods in search of Boisy Long, some Black families came to Fannie Dudley for protection, and were granted it.[146] They were most likely valued servants and longtime tenants who sought sanctuary from the vengeful mob for themselves, and for their families. Their motives were pure survival, but their actions would contribute to a rift in the Black community in Jonesville that would last a hundred years.

There were also rifts in the white community, even in the extended family of Deputy George Wynne. As of ten that morning, with the murder of James Dennis by deputies, the mob lost any

---

144   ibid
145   ibid
146   Ben Pickard with Sally Morrison, *Dudley Farm, A History of Florida Farm Life*, Alachua Press, 2003

semblance of justice and proved itself unreasoning and irrational, capable of turning on anyone, Black or white, who defied them.

J. A. "Dixie" Jones, the son of J. J. Jones for whom Jonesville was named, was Ben Dudley's first cousin. Jones owned the Jones farm directly south of Dudley, where Boisy Long was born. According to a direct descendant, Jones walked the floor all day and night, terrified that Long would come to him for assistance, and the mob would turn their eye on him in vengeance.[147]

Indeed, members of the mob itself were not immune to fear or bad conscience. Some had second thoughts about going through with the lynching after their wives had sent word that they should set the captives, at least the women, free.

According to the African-American community of Jonesville, a Black man in attendance, one well-regarded in the Newberry community, reminded them that the prisoners, including the women, were witnesses. They knew who the mob participants were, and what they'd done, and could identify them if they were freed.[148]

The fear of identification convinced the doubters to assent to the mass lynching, which took place at two on Saturday morning, a time likely chosen as it was the one-day anniversary of Deputy Wynne's shooting. By the light of torches and automobile headlights, two hundred men, including deputies and one state senator, took the prisoners to the shallow sink east of town where Jack Long was hanged in 1909. Though no record of the 1916 mob's *exact* actions remains, it is likely the lynching followed the template that was used in Long's hanging five years before. A "judge" was appointed to sentence the prisoners, and a moment allowed for them to repent and "prepare to meet their Maker."

At some point, the mock court was interrupted when a handful of local high school boys was detected, spying from the trees. Unlike the Dennis family, these witnesses were not killed, but only made

147   Unnamed source, 2013
148   Reverend Willie Mayberry, Jonesville, 2016

to touch the lynching rope, so they too would be implicated in the murders, and tied by the same oath of silence.[149]

Robert Wells, who was then a railroad warden and would in 1929 beat Sheriff Ramsey in a close election for Alachua County sheriff, set the nooses. Myrtle, who said that "two or three of them (the mob members) told her how they done it"[150] described the action of the lynching. "They took [two men] and put a man [each] on two horses, one to go one way and one to go the other,"[151] indicating that Andrew McHenry and Gilbert Dennis were hanged simultaneously, then Mary Dennis and Stella Young afterwards.

When Stella Young was hanged, it was said that the clouds cleared and the moon shone for a moment, lighting the hammock and giving the mob of white men a momentary shock.[152]

News accounts mention that not a single gun was fired, and Frank Dudley bragged that "it was a fine job that was done, as good as a legal lynching, with the necks broke real clean."[153]

Both Dudley and the press conspicuously omit the fact that it was also cold-blooded, premeditated murder, made the more shameful when you consider that sisters were made to watch their brothers hang before their own murders.

It was the *definition* of terror.

***

The horror of the night was not finished when the victims were dead. Two guards were posted to prevent the corpses from being

---

149   ibid
150   Myrtle Dudley, Oral History Interview with Lisa Heard, February 25, 1992, pg. 10, Samuel Proctor Oral History Program Collection, P.K. Yonge Library of Florida History, University of Florida.
151   Myrtle Dudley, Oral History Interview with Lisa Heard, February 25, 1992, pg. 39, Samuel Proctor Oral History Program Collection, P.K. Yonge Library of Florida History, University of Florida.
152   Claudia Aiden, *Gainesville Sun*, "The Newberry Six," September 4, 2005
153   Ron Sachs, Sunday Magazine, "Conspiracy of Silence Shrouds 1916 Lynching," *Gainesville Sun*, November 7, 1977

cut down. Instead, the dead were left to hang in a ruthless sign of vengeance and contempt.[154] William Barry, Sr., who was a first-hand witness, said the bodies were discovered at first light, hanging from the limbs of the same live oak, visible from the Gainesville Road.[155]

The stringer reporters on hand were quick to pen bold-face headlines that appeared in newspapers across the country: ALL THE COUNTRY UP IN ARMS,[156] and RACE WAR OPENS IN NEWBERRY WOMEN LYNCHED,[157] FIVE BLACKS HANGED TO OAK TREE BY MOB OF TWO HUNDRED AT NEWBERRY.[158]

Figure 26. Headlines from 1916

The explosive headlines drew a wave of lynching-tourists to the Newberry picnic grounds. They came from the surrounding

---

154   Myrtle Dudley, Oral History Interview with Lisa Heard, February 25, 1992, pg. 9, Samuel Proctor Oral History Program Collection, P.K. Yonge Library of Florida History, University of Florida.
155   ibid
156   *The Ocala Evening Star*, August 19, 1916
157   The Palm Beach Post, August 20, 1916
158   *Tampa Bay Times*, August 20, 1916

communities by wagon, mule and automobile, to view the mob's handiwork. The crowd, estimated at over a thousand, was mostly white men but included black men, white women and a not a few children.

Spectacle lynching was just that, and the tourists who braved the poor roads and August heat to visit the hammock didn't just hurry by for a quick glimpse, but made a day of it, milling around the picnic grounds with holiday leisure. Dora Jones, a daughter of J. A. Jones, who was six years old at the time, recalled being close enough to the hanging corpses that she and other children were able to push them back and forth in play, like swings on a playground.[159]

The bodies were left to hang until mid-afternoon, when they were cut down, possibly timed to coincide with the return by train of the family who had attended Deputy Wynne's funeral in Quitman. Reporters were still in attendance, and at some point in the afternoon, there is strong evidence that at least two photographs were taken of crowds surrounding the piled corpses, boldly and unashamedly, with no faces masked—there was no need for deception.

The photographs were unearthed by Dr. Marvin Dunn, who found them in the bowels of the Jacksonville Public Library. The words "Lake City" are stamped on their back, and for several years they were thought to have been taken at a mass lynching there in 1911. However, the Lake City lynching victims were riddled with bullets before they were cut down, the mob firing on their corpses for *half an hour*. They were butchered beyond recognition, according to news accounts of the day.[160]

The lynching victims in the photograph Dr. Dunn recovered are clearly not mutilated to that extent, their jackets and clothes intact. In every way they better fit the criteria of the Newberry mass lynching, as remembered by first-hand witnesses.[161]

---

159   Unnamed source, 2014
160   *The Palatka News and Advertiser,* May 26, 1911.
161   As noted by Patricia Hilliard-Nunn: if these photographs *aren't* of the Newberry mass lynching, then there was another mass lynching in North Florida that hasn't yet come to light.

The photographs of the mob weren't in themselves considered outlandish, as the public display of the corpse was an established part of the lynching ritual. Exhibition of the bodies was meant to make an example of them, to show the consequences of breaking the social code. As the technology of photography improved in the twentieth century, mob photographs became commonplace. They were usually too graphic to appear in the newspaper, but were subsequently sold as souvenirs or printed as postcards.[162]

The two photographs thought to be taken at Newberry were not taken at the actual moment of lynching in the pre-dawn hours of Saturday morning, but later in the afternoon, either at Lynch Hammock in Newberry, or possibly at a point along the Old Gainesville Road, as a wagon wheel is pictured in the background, and a cypress or long leaf pine tree. Myrtle Dudley reported that her brother Frank came upon corpses at the "end of the lane."[163] She was being interviewed at her home at Dudley farm, and seems to indicate the lane that ran north and south beside the house, a shortcut to their Aunt Minerva's house in Forest Grove.

If the corpses Frank Dudley saw were indeed the ones in the photograph, which seems likely, it would indicate that the corpses were transported to Dudley property and displayed there after they were cut down. They were eventually buried properly at the cemetery at Pleasant Plain, which is along the same stretch of the Old Gainesville Road.

---

162   Examples of mob photographs at spectator lynching, and a thorough examination of the practice, can be found in James Allen's *Without Sanctuary: Lynching Photography in America,* Twin Palms, 2000

163   Myrtle Dudley, Oral History Interview with Lisa Heard, February 25, 1992, pg. 10, Samuel Proctor Oral History Program Collection, P.K. Yonge Library of Florida History, University of Florida.

Figure 27. Courtesy of the Collection of Marvin Dunn

The first photograph is a close-up of six Black corpses. Though no sure identifications have been made of the bodies, the two older men in the back are possibly J. J. Baskins and Gilbert Dennis; the younger men James Dennis, Andrew McHenry and an unidentified Black man. In the center of the corpses, almost hidden, is the face of a single woman, her wrist still knotted in a rope.

Nine well-dressed white men are posed behind them, standing so close to the corpses that they are nearly standing on their coats. The photographer either lowered the camera to shield these white men's identities, or a more revealing photograph was judiciously cropped to conceal their faces. They are possibly the ringleaders, the "men in automobiles" who inflicted the worst violence, and though the angle of the photograph makes all attempts to identify them purely speculative, it is possible this group included well-placed political leaders.

Frank Dudley passionately declared that "the best men in the district" were in attendance, and though Sidney J. Catts was never officially associated with the Newberry lynching, he had strong friends and allies in the area. Mayor Wallace Cheves, the editor of the *Newberry Miner*, had penned a long endorsement of Catts just weeks before,[164] and Catts himself was known to be in the area that weekend in his "Ford Flivver," beating the bushes of rural North Florida for election support.

The week of August 18, 1918 was a particularly inflamed week in Catts' candidacy, when he was seething over the recount called by Knotts and supported by the Democratic Party, that would eventually give Knotts the nomination. Catts would eventually change parties and win the Florida governorship as the nominee of the Prohibition Party. His near-miraculous win would come largely due to the support he garnered in the rural districts of North and West Florida, though that was months in the future.

During the week of the lynching, Catts was feeling fairly set upon after the Florida Supreme court ruled against him,[165] and ordered a recount, spiraling the candidate into a spate of fiery speeches. On the night of August 18, he gave an explosive speech an hour away at the Ocala bandshell, where he not only attacked Catholics, but the morals of modern womanhood, using such strong language that even his supporters were appalled. An historic supporter of vigilante action, Catts promised that if the Florida Supreme Court gave the nomination to Knotts, he would lead "an army of ten thousand men to Tallahassee and seize the governor's office."[166] Such broad threats of terrorism seemed to play well in the farming communities and phosphate mining towns of north Marion County, where the *Tampa Tribune* deemed Catts had made "a good impression throughout this section."[167]

---

164   *Miami News*, August 2, 1916; *Tampa Tribune*, July 30, 1916
165   *The Andalusia Star*, August 18, 1916
166   *Orlando Evening Star,* August 22, 1916
167   *Tampa Tribune*, August 24, 1916

One wonders if that good impression included a visit to a well-publicized Newberry lynching. In keeping with the oath of silence, no word of his attendance made the papers, but Catts did remind his audiences of his history as a racial enforcer in the weeks to come, so much so that later in that week, the *St. Petersburg Times* penned a thoughtful reproach that was reprinted in the *Ocala Evening Star*. "Rev. Catts may have been justified as he claims, when he 'killed a nigger,' but it is not rather horrible to think of a governor of our state having done such a thing, nevertheless?"[168]

Figure 28. Courtesy of the collection of Marvin Dunn

The second mob photograph is less cautious. It's a broad shot of thirty-five men and boys boldly posed around the strewn bodies of at least five Black corpses. Stella Young, or possibly one of the Dennis sisters, is visible in the center of the corpses, her face upward, her eyes open. The faces of the other victims aren't visible—just their bodies and bare feet, strewn in the dirt, the ropes still encircling their wrists.

168   *The Ocala Evening Star*, September 1, 1916

Several of the white men in the photograph have been identified, most notably the Dudley brothers, who stand on the right end of the front row. Ralph Dudley is standing with his hands together, wearing an oversized suit and straw boater. Frank Dudley is to his right, a young teen in a porkpie hat, still in knee pants. Next to him is Norman Dudley, in a suit, his arms crossed on his chest, his hat aslant. Harvey Dudley stands beside him, in profile, his hat pushed back on his head, his hands on his hips as he stares at the bodies.

Sheriff Ramsey is on the extreme left, in a suit and tie, his hat pulled close on his brow. Senator Daniel Gibbs Roland stands in the center, in a white vest and straw boater, and deputies in bowler hats can be seen on the far right edge of the crowd. Other men in the photograph include Jonesville farmers, phosphate mining supervisors, relatives of George Wynne, and a scattering of Newberry merchants. Several young men are in the group; possibly among them the high schoolers who crashed the lynching and were made to touch the rope.

Every man in the photograph is dressed in his Sunday best, in straw boater hats, suits and watch chains. Harvey Dudley's face is in profile, and inscrutable. The faces of his younger brothers are solemn and aggrieved, as would be expected of young men who have lost their favorite uncle, and now are posed in front of the decomposing corpses of neighbors they'd known their entire lives.

More disconcerting are the faces of the grown men around them. The usual excuse for the lynching of 1916—one perpetuated by both Frank and Myrtle Dudley—is that the friends of Deputy George Wynne were so grief-crazed by his death that they lashed out in their pain, and committed crimes of passion.

The men in the photo do not look crazed by grief.

If anything, they look defiant, staring into the eye of history without insight and without pity, the corpses of a murdered family at their feet.

Chapter Eight

THE CAPTURE OF BOISY LONG

The capture of Boisy Long on Sunday evening, August 20, 1916, was presented in the press as a cut-and-dried moment of extreme good luck on behalf of the Alachua County sheriff's department. According to the *Ocala Evening Star*, Long randomly approached an "old colored preacher" named Squire Long at his farm seven miles northeast of Newberry in the Bennington Section, and asked for food.[169] *The Tampa Tribute* parsed out a slightly longer narrative, that Boisy Long asked for food the first night and was given it by Squire Long, who did not recognize him. [170]

According to the *Tribune's* version, Boisy Long was "much jaded because of lack of food," and returned the next evening to ask for more help. This time, Squire Long recognized him as a fugitive and with the help of his son, Jackson, immediately turned Boisy Long over to Sheriff Ramsey, at the curiously recurring hour of two in the morning, to the relief and approbation of all. "The action of the old negro, Squire Long, is [*sic*] bringing the murderer to the Gainesville jail was very unusual, very sensible, and can't be too highly commended."[171]

169   *The Ocala Evening Star*, August 21, 1916
170   *The Tampa Tribune*, August 22, 1916
171   ibid

The accounts made for a tidy ending and a compelling bit of storytelling. Squire Long's portrayal as a "wise old colored preacher" reduced his part in Boisy Long's arrest to recognizable elements for the digestion of white readers—the story of the negro desperado being apprehended, against all expectation, by a wise old member of his own tribe. According to the rules of blood-law, such a transaction would return harmony to the region—a member of the offending tribe offering up the life of the offender.

That was possibly the underlying storyline that law enforcement hoped to convey, post-lynching, though many of the details were deliberate lies. In truth, Squire Long was not an elderly old preacher, but younger by three years than Deputy Wynne. Boisy Long's appearance at his door was not random, and it is doubtful they were strangers, as their families had many connections to Black Jonesville.

Squire Long's mother, Flora Long, owned land in Jonesville in 1900 near Dudley, the closest store, and the Dennis/Long/McHenry families, who were only separated by a few houses. *The Crisis* reported that Squire Long was, in fact, Boisy Long's uncle, a relationship that was denied by the family as a matter of survival.[172] The connection better explains why Boisy Long would have sought him out for assistance, as Squire Long was a prominent preacher, healer and farmer. In essence, he was a figure well-known in every generation of Southern life, the aspiring uncle born in modest circumstances who'd done well for himself.

Boisy Long, who was wounded in his arm, would have had to have traveled the seven miles to his uncle's farm by foot, where family members say he hid in the fields, as the Tampa paper reported. For Squire Long to fail to recognize him seems unlikely, as members of the posse had visited Squire Long and, according to *The Crisis*, had terrorized him.[173]

Squire Long, if he did know Boisy was hiding in his fields, didn't

---

172   *The Crisis*, "Another Lynching," October 1916
173   ibid

turn him in immediately, but allowed a two-day lag, until the odd hour of two Sunday morning, the second anniversary of Deputy Wynne's shooting, and the first anniversary of the mass lynching. The timing might suggest Squire Long was given an ultimatum, along with a time-limit.

**

As Boisy Long hid out in his uncle's field, high tension was gathering in downtown Newberry where white Newberrians found themselves challenged by "several hundred" Black miners. The *Florida-Times Union* mentioned their presence in the area on Saturday when reporting the details of the lynching, noting that the miners were "rough in the extreme, and killings have been numerous."[174]

A day later, *The Atlanta Constitution* reported, "When news of the lynching here reached the phosphate mines today, a large number of Negros gathered in town and for a time it was feared a race war would result. White men seized all available arms and ammunition, and after a short time, the Negros dispersed."[175] [176]

The exact origin, and indeed, the fate of these Black miners has been almost completely lost to history, though Black resistance to white bullying was not unheard of in phosphate country. Seventeen years before, in one county south in Dunnellon, Black miners had formed an armed organization—The Dunnellon Anti-Lynch and Mob Club—that had succeeded in thwarting at least two lynchings.[177] The organization was soon crushed by law enforcement—including

---

174   *The Florida-Times Union*, August 19, 1916
175   *The Atlanta Constitution*, August 20, 1916
176   The fear of race war wasn't new in Alachua County. A militia company called The Gainesville Minutemen had been raised in 1859, to quell any local hint of slave rebellion after John Brown's raid at Harper's Ferry, Virginia.
177   *Emancipation Betrayed, The Hidden History of Black Organizing and White Violence in Florida from Reconstruction to the Bloody Election of 1920*, Paul Ortiz, 2005

Alachua County deputies—but the memory of their armed resistance was not forgotten.

In response to the uprising in downtown Newberry, "the whites corralled all the ammunition that was in the stores and prepared for trouble."[178] The gathering of the ammunition put the odds on the side of the white men, who had friends and allies far beyond the city limits of Newberry. Their ability to hold the train in Waldo and bring Robert Wells to town on a few hours' notice, demonstrates their close connections with not only statewide law enforcement, but dominant corporate concerns like Dutton, Cummer, and the all-powerful Atlantic-Coastal Railroad.

Few details remain of the engagement, though Myrtle Dudley certainly feared retaliation. "I do not ever want to live through anything like this community was for about ten days. At sundown, every door on every house was shut just as tight as they could shut them. They were afraid that the niggers were going to team together and get them."[179]

Myrtle's fears weren't unfounded. As protection, the Archer Night Riders were said to have "willingly worked all four corners of Alachua County without hesitation, protecting family members and property perimeters."[180]

Myrtle also speculated that there were more Black casualties after the lynching than were ever reported. "I think there were twenty-five or thirty nigras killed out here in the woods. And not a white man in among them . . . . That was pure nigra."[181]

Whether this high number is body-count bragging (Myrtle

---

178   *The Florida Times-Union*, August 18, 1916
179   Myrtle Dudley, Oral History Interview with Lisa Heard, February 25, 1992, pg. 11, Samuel Proctor Oral History Program Collection, P.K. Yonge Library of Florida History, University of Florida.
180   Lizzie PRB Jenkins, *Black America Series Alachua County Florida*, Arcadia Press
181   Myrtle Dudley, Oral History Interview with Lisa Heard, February 25, 1992, pg. 40, Samuel Proctor Oral History Program Collection, P.K. Yonge Library of Florida History, University of Florida.

was prone) or evidence of other casualties, possibly from conflict between the miners and the white mob, is not known.

Given the nine miles between Squire Long's farm in Bennington and downtown Newberry, Squire Long might not have known about the miner uprising gathering there on Saturday night. What he *did* know, unequivocally, was his own fate if he was suspected of assisting nephew Boisy Long in any way—a public, violent death, not only for him, but possibly his entire household, including his seventy-six-year-old mother.

The mob had demonstrated its willingness to kill noncombatants, including women. *The Crisis* asserted that Squire Long did not voluntarily hand Boisy Long over, but had been visited by the mob and terrorized even before Boisy showed up at his door.[182]

It's also possible that Boisy's surrender was a negotiated arrangement between Squire Long and Sheriff Ramsey. Both were successful farmers within the vast reaches of the old Arredondo grant, and almost certainly knew each other. Squire Long's standing in the community might have been such that he was able to parlay safe passage for Boisy if he turned him in—a promise from the Sheriff that the fugitive would not be subject to the grisly death that the mob would mete out if they caught him first.

Without such assurance, Boisy Long had no hope of a clean lynching, but instead would expect one that included mutilation and torture, something Sheriff Ramsey had hinted would happen when he told reporters that he "feared for the life of the Black if he fell into the hands of the searchers."[183]

There is also a story that has been passed down in Black Jonesville for a hundred years—that Squire Long did not take Boisy Long by force. According to this account, Boisy hid in his uncle's fields for a day. When he finally knocked on his door on Saturday night, Squire sat him down and told him about the shooting of James Dennis, and

---

182   *The Crisis*, "Another Lynching," October 1916
183   *The Tampa Tribune*, August 19, 1916

the lynching of his wife, cousins and in-laws, whose hanging bodies had remained all day in Newberry for the amusement of the tourists.

Squire Long was said to have spelled out the reality of the situation to his nephew, telling him that it would either be his life or the lives of Squire's family, and that Boisy Long had voluntarily turned himself in to end the bloodshed.

Which of these scenarios played out—possibly a bit of all of them—is unknown. What *is* known is that in the early morning hours of Sunday, August 20, 1916, Squire and his son, Jackson Long, delivered Boisy Long to the custody of Sheriff P. G. Ramsey in Gainesville. There does seem to be a scent of negotiation in the deal, as Boisy's treatment thereafter was strikingly less barbaric.

Sheriff Ramsey, who was reportedly present (and possibly the shooter of James Dennis), became suddenly committed to the absolute safety of the man he had so assiduously pursued. He feared the mob would "most surely" take Boisy Long if he were kept in the Gainesville jail, and thus spirited Long, Mills Dennis and another prisoner, Will Turner, to a secret location for safekeeping, later identified as the Jacksonville jail. They were accompanied by several deputies and County Solicitor William Long, to the jail of W. H. Dowling.[184]

The extreme security used in the transfer marks a change in the tone of the weekend: the fury of blood-revenge was overtaken by the rule of law. The capricious destruction of the Black community, which would follow similar lynchings in Rosewood and Perry, did not happen in Jonesville, nor were any further murders committed— or at least none known to present record.

Sheriff Ramsey was able to regain control of his county in a way that Sheriff Elias Walker could not, five years later in Rosewood. How Ramsey regained that power—by violence or by parley—is not known, but was almost certainly was connected to the surrender of Boisy Long.

---

184   *The Miami News*, August 23, 1916

Chapter Nine

UNCIVILIZED AND
UNFAVORABLE BUSINESS

W ith the capture of Boisy Long, the escalating violence of the weekend began a precipitous decline. The bodies of Gilbert and Mary Dennis, Stella Young, Andrew McHenry and Joshua Baskins were released to their families, and at least three of them, possibly all, were buried in the shaded cemetery behind Pleasant Plain Methodist Church, two miles northeast of the Dudley homestead.

The graves of James Dennis, Andrew McHenry, and Joshua Baskins still stand in the old cemetery, though they are worn with the years, and Dennis' tombstone is badly damaged. There are over seventy unmarked/

Figure 29. James Dennis' grave at Pleasant Plain. Damaged stone makes inscription illegible except for last word: "blessed."

unknown graves at Pleasant Plain, and it is thought that Stella Young and Mary Dennis are also buried there in unmarked graves.

With the arrest of Boisy Long, the reversal in attitude among local editors was significant. Newspapers that howled outrage on Friday seem chastised and reasonable on Monday, with a few perverse attempts at humor to leaven the horror of the weekend, such as the quip in *The Tampa Tribune* on August 22. "Those Newberry fellows are not pikers. They lynch them in bunches of five."

Figure 30. Andrew McHenry's grave at Pleasant Plain. The worn inscription reads "Sleep and rest thy rest is in heaven."

More grievous, and typical of the day, was the tongue-in-cheek account of a grand jury finding that appeared in the *Ocala Evening Star* that poked grotesque fun at the manner of the victims' deaths, reporting on the "remarkable verdict" the coroner's jury found. "The jury seems to have investigated seven deaths. One negro man, according to the reported coroner's verdict, came to his death by running into a barbed wire fence and cutting himself to death. Another man came to his death by smashing his head against a telephone post. Two women fell out of a tree and choked to death. Three men, who had climbed into the tree to rescue the women, fell out and broke their necks."[185]

This macabre post represents the callousness and the mockery that was elemental in the race wars of the turn of the century

---

185   *Ocala Evening Star,* August 19, 1916

where the basest murders—of a family, and women—were not only condoned, but often given the late-night-comedian treatment. Such ribaldry telegraphed to readers that the newspaper might fall in line and report the lynching as unlawful, but only while giving a wink-wink at the absurdity of anyone taking the loss of Black lives too seriously.

The editor who penned the piece had obviously been given inside information by one of the "men in the automobiles," who were eyewitnesses of the abductions as well as the lynching. They were most likely describing the hanging of Stella Young and Mary Dennis at the hammock, the two women who "fell out of the tree," as well as the lynching of Andrew McHenry, J. J. Baskins, and Gilbert Dennis, the three men who climbed into the tree to "rescue the women, fell out and broke their necks." The other details probably describe the capture of J. J. Baskins or Gilbert Dennis, who might have run into barbed wire while trying to escape, and the shooting of James Dennis, whose head wound was said to have made by his accidental collision with a nearby telegraph post.

Notably absent from the quip is any mention of James Dennis' children, who witnessed their father's abduction and heard the shot that killed him. It would have been hard, even in 1916, to put a jokey spin on that bit of inhumanity.

The Ocala editor's facetious take on the matter was commonplace, but not universal. The men of the mob and their friends in power could explain and excuse, and even make joking fun of the entire ordeal, but the lynching of a family, including two women, while not unknown, was a serious matter, not easily explained away. According to Joel Buchannon, one of the men of the mob was so conscience-stricken that he eventually paid for the education of some of the victims' children to atone for his participation.

The Stark Telegraph didn't make light of the matter, but offered a quiet rebuke. "We have had too much of this uncivilized and unfavorable business in Florida recently. It is disturbing to us at home and harmful abroad. Let's get back to enlightenment and progress."[186]

The combination of shame and fear of a race riot, and possibly a promise by Sheriff Ramsey to try Boisy Long according to by-the-book legal standards, took the matter out of the lawlessness of mob rule and put it firmly in the hands of the court in Gainesville.

A special term of court was called for September 6, three weeks after the bodies were cut down, a concession by the state that was offered to the still-seething friends of Deputy Wynne, to assure them justice would be swiftly carried out. When the all-white grand jury convened at the Gainesville courthouse, Judge J. T. Willis "spoke on the importance of legally handling such cases as Long's and in his charge to the grand jury laid special stress against summary justice."[187]

The grand jury had other ideas, and after duly studying the evidence, made a grave and thoughtful statement "deploring the acts of violence that have recently been committed in our county." They assured the court that they had diligently investigated "with a view of ascertaining the guilty parties" but were unable to affix guilt. They went on to recommend that people look to the authorities to solve and punish crime, and "refrain from such acts of violence as casts a reflection upon this, our county."[188]

The report offered little solace to the families of the lynching victims and only confirmed what they suspected would happen: nothing. The machinery of law and order were weak weapons when faced with the twin cabals of big business and tribal loyalty. The dramatic wording of the finding, along with the lack of substance, made the grand jury statement so hollow that it almost reads as parody, except for the last line which seems more sincerely voiced—a

---

186   *The Stark Telegraph*, untitled, August 23, 1916
187   *Tampa Bay Times*, "Boisy Long On Trial For Life," September 8, 1916
188   William Wilbanks, *Forgotten Heroes: Police Officers Killed in Early Florida, 1840-1925*, 1998

reminder that the rest of Alachua County did not want to be stuck with the lawless reputation that threatened any semblance of an economic rebound on the West End.

***

The grand jury investigation into the death of George Wynne had far less difficulty returning a murder indictment against Boisy Long. On September 5, a special term of court was called before Judge J. T. Willis. Robert E. Davis was appointed Long's attorney, with A.V. Long the prosecuting attorney.[189] The trial was held on September 7, at the courthouse in Gainesville in front of twelve white jurors.

Grady Blount took the stand to testify about the shooting that had happened in Jonesville less than three weeks before, as did Lem Harris and Tom Wynne, who testified that his brother had regained consciousness on the train ride to Jacksonville on Friday morning, long enough to tell him, "Tom, I am going to die. Boisy Long has shot me."[190]

His testimony was apparently not challenged, but was contrary to the memories of Katie Bea Cooke, whose Uncle Henry drove George Wynne to the train: he reported that Wynne lost consciousness on the Gainesville Highway and never regained it.

A Jacksonville doctor testified about George Wynne's injuries, and Boisy Long took the stand to offer his own account of the night. He described a scenario almost identical to the state's case, except that in his telling, at that tense moment of arrest when he was picked up his pistol to get to his shirt, Deputy Wynne pulled first.

The entire trial took less than two and a half hours. The lawyers made their cases, the witnesses testified, and the jury[191] deliberated

---

189   ibid
190   ibid
191   The jurors were: F. W. Tyson, C. C. Sherouse, H. C. Forsyth, G. A. Wiggins (foreman), L. A. Sherouse, E. A. Flowers, B. W. Waits, W. F. Beckham, F. O. Parker, J. W. Sherouse, C. F. Morrison, and R. M. Chamberlin. (6)

for seven minutes before they found Boisy Long guilty in the standard language of the day. "Thursday September 7, 1916. And thereafter on the same day returned into court and rendered the following verdict to wit: We the Jury find the defendant guilty of murder in the first degree so say we all."[192]

Governor Park Trammell signed the warrant for Long's execution on October 13, with the execution date set for Friday, October 27. There were no delays or challenges to his sentence, and Long was hanged on the yard of the Alachua County jail by Sheriff P. G. Ramsey on October 27, when hangings were still open to the public.

An editor with *The Gainesville Sun* commented on the crowd who attended the hanging, which was apparently well attended. "[A] bigger crowd than a church revival, a political meeting, or even a barbecue. Men will go many miles in order to see some poor devil, whose atrocious crime has put him under the curse of the law, fall from the end of a rope, struggle and die, when they would not walk two blocks to learn the way of eternal life." The editor asked cryptically, "Why is this?"[193]

Though no names were included, it is likely many of the members of the mob who had terrorized the West End on August 18 put on their suits and boaters and attended Boisy Long's execution with the same satisfaction with which they'd presided over the murder of his family members.

---

192   Alachua County Court Records, September 7, 1916
193   *The Ocala Evening Star*, Untitled, October 30, 1916

Chapter Ten

LOOKING TO RELOCATE

T he oath of silence taken by the mob could not erase the memory of the weekend of August 18. There were too many witnesses, and too much publicity, including the reporter who was sent from *The Crisis*, who wrote under the byline M. A. H.

Unlike the stringer reporters who'd hopped the train to Newberry and wired in similar, sometimes cannibalized stories, *The Crisis* reporter came as a seasoned investigator. Whether M. A. H. was female or male, Black or white, is not noted on the article, but the voice of the piece is that of the *New Negro*—brisk, strident, and absolutely fed up, in every sense of the word, with white lynch mobs.

M. A. H's firsthand assessment of the lynching appeared in the October 1916 edition and was titled *Another Lynching*. The article offered a Black perspective of Jonesville and Newberry that was strikingly different from that of the white reporters, in almost every way.

Black Jonesville farmers who were dismissed and reviled in the white press as thieves and desperados, were presented in *The Crisis* as they appear in the census—as nothing more or less than small-holding farmers who were struggling, but making their way in hard economic times.

M. A. H. was far from impressed by the civic upgrades undertaken by the City of Newberry, which they described with painful honesty as "a desolate place of shanties and small houses and has a reputation for lawlessness. There is not one good building in the place and many of the houses are vacant. The sun beats down on the roofs and there is almost no shade."[194]

An opinion piece that ran in the same edition, almost certainly penned by the great W. E. B. Dubois himself, did not spare the feelings of either the white or the Black communities of Newberry and Jonesville. If possible, Black Jonesville got the worse of it.

Dubois seethed that they "acted like a set of cowardly sheep. Without resistance they let a white mob whom they outnumbered two to one, torture, harry and murder their women, shoot down innocent men entirely unconnected with the alleged crime, and finally to cap the climax, they caught and surrendered the wretched man whose attempted arrest caused the difficulty."[195]

Dubois concluded that they forfeited the sympathy of civilized folk, and that the Black community should have "fought in self-defense to the last ditch if they had killed every white man in the county and themselves been killed." He recommended that, "The man who surrendered to a lynching mob, the victim of the sheriff, ought himself to been locked up."[196]

The anguished rage of *The Crisis* is understandable, but was misdirected concerning the Black community of the West End, which *did* rise up to challenge the lynching. Black miners did gather and confront the mob, but to what extent and to what end is unknown.

Their resistance did not end in violence, but the fact that it was even offered was no doubt a shocking challenge to the influential corporations that depended on their labor. It was a sacrifice that went unheralded, and grievously underreported.

---

194   *The Crisis*, "Another Lynching," October, 1916
195   *The Crisis*, "Cowardice," October 1916
196   ibid

The stinging rebuke in *The Crisis*, which was published nationwide to a readership of nearly 100,000, was surely salt in the wounds of the Black farmers of Jonesville, who were still grieving the loss of three well-loved families, and making arrangements to raise their orphaned toddlers and children. They were already split over the circumstances of Boisy Long's arrest, and saw betrayal on one side and furious condemnation on the other.

Though white Newberry seemed from the outside to solidly support the lynching, there were voices of dissent, even in 1916, when such talk might be construed as "asking for a killin." A white preacher that Frank Dudley alludes to but does not name, was threatened into silence after condemning the lynching. A white Western Union Telegraph line man named L. A. Madden was "requested by citizens to leave town" by people "not prepared to listen to his intemperate utterances."[197]

Other men who were close to the action left soon afterward, including Harvey Dudley, who went to Texas to work on a ranch— possibly with his Uncle Fred, who lived in Tarrant County. He returned to Newberry to enlist and serve in World War I, and at the end of the war did not return to Dudley, but worked as a mail clerk in Jacksonville for the remainder of his life.[198] Other men left without explanation, including Dr. Huff, several Dudley nephews, and two county deputies. Society columns in local newspapers report other businessmen from Newberry arriving in Ocala and Tampa the week after the lynching, under the mild heading, "Looking to Relocate."

Though these "relocations" were couched in the polite language of the day, there is no doubt that some of the men moved due to fear of arrest, or retaliation, or any entanglement in the trial, or aftermath.[199] Between 1910 and 1920, the town's population dropped by almost

---

197   *The Ocala Evening Star*, "Madden Had to Move," August 22, 1916
Madden's criticism of Deputy Wynne was not related to the lynching, *per se*, but connected to his previous arrest by Wynne.
198   *Dudley Farm, a History of Florida Farm Life*, Alachua Press, 2003
199   ibid

half, from roughly 1,500 to 800. The closing of the mines was the foremost factor in the decline, but the lynching was a contributor.

To the families who had built the nice homes in the downtown, and who worked in professions already strained by the economic downturn, the lynching of women and the public display of their corpses was the last straw, an incomprehensibly barbaric act that confirmed their fears about the West End as a rough and lawless place.

The outward movement of population was accelerated in April when America entered the European War, and young men twenty-one to thirty-one were registered to serve. Lem Harris, who had recovered from his hand wounds, was a sympathetic figure to county leaders. He was appointed to work for Selective Service and registered Newberry men for the draft. You'll see his signature penned on many a Newberry draft card, along with the name, occupation, hair color and build of just about every young man in the district.

World War I dug deeply into the farms of the West End, depriving them of essential labor, including the sons who would have traditionally taken over family farms on their father's death. Three of the Dudley brothers served: Norman Dudley was badly wounded in the trenches and left the war with significant post-traumatic stress. Frank Dudley was the only son who did not serve, and he was readying himself to report to service when the war ended.[200]

The bitter racial divide in the rural communities around the Big Bend wasn't dissipated by the war, though the practice of lynching was (finally) condemned by President Woodrow Wilson in a speech made in July 1918, that drew a firm line. "I say plainly that every American who takes part in the action of a mob or gives it any sort of countenance is no true son of this great democracy, but its betrayer."[201]

His strong words, long overdue, were largely ignored in the

---

200   *Dudley Farm, a History of Florida Farm Life*
201   *The Miami News*, July 26, 1918

rural counties of North Florida, where violence flared back to life when Black soldiers returned home with combat experience and the expectation of better treatment by the country they'd served. In 1920, there were race riots in Ocoee after Black men tried to vote, where two white men and five Black men were killed, and most of the Black section of town burned down.

In 1922, two counties away in Perry, connected to Newberry by a daily train, a Black man named Charles Wright was accused of the murder of a white schoolteacher. The local public schools, including small children, were let out to watch as he was burned at the stake. Afterwards, two more Black men were lynched, and essential buildings in the Black community were burned.

Even closer to home, next door in Levy County, was the burning of Rosewood in 1921, after a white woman accused a Black man of assault, triggering a week of violence when at least eight people were killed—two white and six Black. Like Perry, Rosewood had many Newberry connections, and it is likely that some of the outsiders who flooded into the woods of Rosewood that cold first week of January were veterans of the mob violence in Newberry five years before.

Figure 31. Ruins in Rosewood, January 1921. Courtesy of Florida Memory

Levy County Sheriff R. E. Walker did not gain control of the situation for days, and in the end called in Sheriff P. G. Ramsey for assistance in quelling the violence. Ramsey served as president of the Florida Sheriff's Association after the Newberry lynching in 1919, and may have been seen as an expert, or at least a man with experience in controlling the flames of mob destruction.

The continued eruptions of mob violence swelled the exodus of Black labor from the rural South from a trickle to a solid wave, creating what would be known as the Great Migration.[202] The loss of essential labor was so massive and economically debilitating in North Florida that even old race-baiters like Sidney J. Catts found themselves backpedaling on their racist rhetoric.

Catts, who had resisted condemning lynching for most of his years in office, began to speak of harmony among the races, though his about-face was too little, too late, in the flat woods of the Big Bend. The lawlessness was too capricious and too expensive. It was bad for business, and when the Cummer sawmill in Sumner burned, the Cummer brothers moved their entire operations from Rosewood and Newberry to Lacoochee, a custom-built company town in Pasco County.

Lewis Abraham, whose father owned a store in Newberry during the 1916 lynching, moved to Lacoochee in 1923. He boasted that workers did not bring the racial violence of the Big Bend with them to Lacoochee. They lived in segregated quarters, but Black and white worked side by side with "no animosity and there was no problem."[203]

***

The loss of the mines and lumber operations created a deficiency of jobs, population and reputation from which the town of Newberry

---

202   For more information on The Great Migration, read Isabel Wilkerson's *The Warmth of Other Suns: The Epic Story of America's Great Migration,* 2010
203   Lewis Abraham (1925-2004) Interview by Dr. Marc Yacht, part of CARES project.

would not recover. The soaring aspirations of Newberry the Boomtown, with trains, access to international money, and steady public improvement was soon nothing more than a memory.

Trains still ran through the downtown, but they were freight, not passenger lines, and no longer dropped off free-spending drummers and phosphate speculators to fill the local boarding houses and hotels. Tourists who passed through town on Highway 41 might stop to buy gas and have a bite to eat, but found no reason to stay.

The diminishing pool of professional jobs were filled by the sons of a handful of white families, related by blood, church and oath, who steadily bought up the cheap farmland for as little as a dime an acre. Cotton was replaced by cattle-ranching, melons, and in the mid-1930s, bright-leaf tobacco. These farming operations did not require the brick-front offices that the departed professional class had built, leaving downtown Newberry a husk of its former self.

The bank, electric light plant, and a handful of churches and small grocers remained, but the high-ceilinged homes of the white professionals suffered a Faulknerian decline, many lost to neglect or fire, the remaining blocks falling into disrepair. The spreading limbs of the oak hammock on the east end of town, once a pleasant shaded field for picnics and political speeches, became a dump with an unpleasant title: "Lynch Hammock."

In the travel guide published by the WPA in 1934, Newberry made a brief appearance, mentioned as a melon-shipping district—nothing more.

The Community of Dudley suffered a similar decline, its growth undercut by the loss of their sons to war, and the boll weevil infestation that deprived them of cotton, their most profitable crop. Ben Dudley died in October of 1918, just weeks after Harvey Dudley shipped overseas. Fannie Dudley survived him by almost twenty years, living at the farm at Dudley and cared for by her daughters, four of whom never married.[204]

---

204   *Dudley Farm, a History of Florida Farm Life,* Alachua Press, 2003.

Only Ralph stayed to farm with his sisters, Edna, Winnie and Myrtle, with the help of hired Black laborers, who required higher wages after the war. When Myrtle was asked if they had trouble keeping the farm running in the Depression, she answered with sour honesty. "No. We had trouble keeping nigras wanting to work for a loaf of bread."[205]

The reluctance of Black laborers to work at Dudley for low wages, or as tenants, had a solid economic impact on the farm's prosperity. Without them, the Community of Dudley slowly lost parcels, sold for cash. The showpiece of a main house was not described from memory of a younger kinsman as a "plantation house," but less poetically and more accurately, as a *haunted* one.[206]

Jonesville fared even worse, as it was unincorporated and completely displaced when Highway 26 did not follow the path of the old Gainesville Highway, but was built slightly south of it. The well-known crossroads at the Community of Dudley was suddenly not a crossroads at all, but a weed-grown private drive. The pond that welcomed cattle drivers at the turn of the century was depleted by agricultural pumping, eventually becoming a dry hole, sometimes mistaken for an abandoned phosphate pit, such as those dotting the woods of the old West End.

When Cummer Lumber moved to Pasco County, their commissary building was rolled on logs to the corner of Highway 26 and Farnsworth Road, making it the new Jonesville Crossroads. The commissary became a feed store (and later an antique mall) that sat across the highway from the Farnsworth gas station, which was called "ten-mile past grocery store" due to its location ten miles west of Gainesville.

For many years, the crossroads at Jonesville and a handful of scattered cemeteries and churches were the only landmarks left of

<hr>

205   Myrtle Dudley, Oral History Interview with Lisa Heard, February 25, 1992, pg. 44, Samuel Proctor Oral History Program Collection, P.K. Yonge Library of Florida History, University of Florida.

206   *Dudley Farm, a History of Florida Farm Life*, Alachua Press, 2003.

Jonesville, which had been one of the county's oldest settlements. Dudley was still there, a quarter mile south of Highway 26, with nothing to mark it but a listing mailbox, shorn of its early-century prominence.

After Ralph Dudley died in 1967, his sisters lived there with Frank nearby, out of sight and out of mind, until 1977 when a young journalist named Ron Sachs tracked down the last of the eyewitnesses of the nearly forgotten lynching, and penned a remarkable piece of in-depth journalism that appeared in the *Sunday Magazine*, an insert in the *Gainesville Sun*, on November 7, 1977.

Sachs, who would have an award-winning career in investigative journalism, interviewed a handful of first-hand witnesses, including Frank Dudley, who at age seventy-seven abandoned caution and discussed the lynching with a front-porch gregariousness, defending the action as "100% right." Dudley insisted the accused were indeed thieves, the women and men both, and were "in for a killin' to end their rougish ways."[207]

Dudley clarified the record as to the location of the lynching, but refused to go on the record with exact locations or name specific names.

"There might still be some living," he said, "but I ain't gonna say so. In another five years or so, there probably won't be anyone left to tell the story firsthand."[208]

Dudley was smugly sure the oath of silence would be maintained, concluding his tale with the assurance, "No one outside here is ever gonna find out. No one is ever going to know the 100 percent truth."[209]

***

Ron Sachs' article must have shaken the windows in Newberry when the newspaper arrived on their doorstep, because Frank Dudley

---

207   Ron Sachs, Sunday Magazine, "Conspiracy of Silence Shrouds 1916 Lynching," *Gainesville Sun*, November 7, 1977
208   ibid
209   ibid

wasn't the only local who spoke on the record. William Barry, Sr., whose family owned the Suwanee Pharmacy where Lem Harris had worked, also spoke with Sachs. Barry tap-danced around his exact role in the lynching and claimed not to know the names of the actual murderers, which is possible in the sense that he didn't see them tie the rope. He does appear to be in the mob photograph—the slight young man in the center row, wearing a porkpie hat. It is possible that he only participated, as he describes to Sachs, as a curious young man following the commotion, and coming upon the bodies hanging on a single oak tree on the morning of August 19.

Barry had served on the Alachua County School Board, and was a leading light in farming and education. He used the same racial phrasing as Frank Dudley did in 1977, which makes for jarring reading. He also did that thing no one in white Newberry had yet attempted; he not only condemned the lynching, but attempted to explain the mindset of the day that had allowed such a thing to happen: "I'm sure more white citizens would agree now that back then, many white people believed that a nigger didn't have a soul. They were mistreated—it was a terrible thing. I don't know who done it, but it was wrong. As far as the community and history go, that was probably our worst day."[210]

Sachs also spoke to a local Black man named R. Henry, the son of a Jonesville farmer who was eleven years old in 1916. Henry was not a witness to the lynching, but his father, Richard Henry, went down to the hammock on Saturday to see what the commotion was about and saw the strung-up bodies.

At age seventy-two, Henry was one of the few, if only, citizens who went on the record to refute the claims that the Dennis family were thieves. "The white folks said all those colored folks was thieves, but it wasn't so. My daddy said it wasn't so."[211]

And finally, Sachs interviewed Murray Randolph, the youngest

---

210   ibid
211   ibid

child of Stella Young and Boisy Long, who was a toddler in 1916. In keeping with the long habit of the Black community in Jonesville, Randolph was terse in discussing the lynching with an outsider.

He said he "grew up hearing all the stories but I don't know any truth except both my parents died. I never really knew them." He also denied being angry about it. "Years ago I might have been mad about it. I don't know who to hold responsible, so I don't. What was done is done."[212]

---

212   ibid

Chapter Eleven

AWAKENINGS

Murray Randolph's stoic acceptance of his parents' deaths was the last word on the Newberry lynching for a very long time. County historians knew of the event and made notations of the lynching victims' names, which were often confused and misspelled, but included in the historic record, if anyone cared to look.

The central role the Dudley family played in the lynching was seldom noted, not as political favor, but simply because the once-prominent family had lost social position in the sixty years after the lynching. They were no longer the area's premier planters, but just one of dozens of small farming operations on the rural western side of Alachua County.

The entire holdings of the old farm might have been torn down and lost to memory if not for a local agriculture agent named Buck Mitchell, who lived and worked in the Newberry area in the early 1980s. One of his jobs was testing cattle for *brucellosis*, and one of the herds he tested was kept in the fields of a ramshackle, old-timey farm that was managed with tart wiliness by a Cracker matriarch in her eighties named Myrtle Dudley.

Myrtle did not suffer fools gladly and was no friend of the state. She had lived her entire life at the farm that her grandfather, Captain

Dudley, had homesteaded before the Civil War. She was infirm, and had let the homestead grow up around her, living mostly in the back side of the listing old house where she had been born. Like all farms, something was always in need of repair, and Myrtle was not above asking for free labor from the "state man."

Mitchell was willing to twist a few bolts and reset cattle troughs, and in time, a friendship sprang up between them. Mitchell was intrigued by the homestead at Dudley, where time seemed frozen, as if under a conjurer's spell. The gable of the dark, tin-roofed house peeked above a swept dirt yard full of wild-running roses Myrtle and her sisters once cultivated. The entire homestead was overgrown with a true Florida tangle of grapevine, fig trees, citrus trees, and fat old cypress that marked the once-significant crossroads.

There was history there, overgrown and swallowed, but certainly not forgotten by Miss Myrtle, who liked to sit on her front porch in the cool of the evening and watch the sun set. She was glad for the company and told Buck Mitchell many charming (and alarming) stories of the Dudleys' long stewardship of the land. She spoke often of her mother, Fannie Dudley, who was a powerful force in all her children's lives, and mentioned that Fannie had wanted to leave the hard-worked homestead to someone who would preserve it, and take care in remembering its past.

Mitchell encouraged her to do so, and in 1982, Myrtle donated the Dudley homestead and twenty-four acres of the farm to the State of Florida, along with furnishings, out-buildings, and papers. The gift was particularly fruitful as Myrtle continued to live at the homestead while the renovations were underway, offering a first-hand witness to the past century. In 1991, she won the Florida Folk Heritage Award in recognition of her contributions to the state.

Figure 32. Myrtle Dudley, 1992. Courtesy of Florida Memory

Myrtle won the award despite never repenting for her family's involvement in the Newberry lynching, continuing to live her life an unfiltered and unrepentant racist. On one occasion, she was hosting a lunch for the park rangers who were working on the restoration of the homestead. When she learned one of the workers was Black, she refused to let him inside her house to eat lunch. In solidarity, all of the rangers ate outside.[213]

The State of Florida allowed Myrtle such liberties, perhaps for the greater good of saving the farm and collecting her folk history. Certainly, the state rangers who worked with Myrtle Dudley understood her racial views, and thanks to Frank Dudley's interview in 1977, also knew the close association between the family and the lynchings.

The official Dudley biography,[214] published in 2003, included a chapter on the lynching, penned in broad strokes, with the onus

---

213   Unnamed source
214   Ben Pickard with Sally Morrison, *Dudley Farm, A History of Florida Farm Life*, Alachua Press, 2003

of guilt put on the members of the anonymous mob. The Dudley family's central role in the lynching was minimized, while the fact that Black neighbors sought "protection and comfort"[215] from Fannie Dudley was included, offering what seems to be an intentionally misleading understanding of the family's role in the event.

To the state's credit is Myrtle's oral history, taken by Lisa Heard and Sally Morrison on February 25, 1992. They encouraged Myrtle to speak freely, which she did, offering an authentic slice of Old Florida in her every breath—her pride of family, distrust of outsiders, and the absolute depth of her racism which was not a fluke of record, but reflected commonly held beliefs of her day.

**

The restoration of the Community of Dudley and near-sanctification of the Dudley family in the park's literature and museum drew the attention of African-American historian and documentarian Dr. Patricia Hilliard-Nunn. A professor of African-American Studies at the University of Florida, Hilliard-Nunn had begun documenting Black history in Alachua County as a filmmaker in the 1990s.

When interviewing Black Alachua County natives, she noted that the 1916 lynching in Jonesville kept coming up in conversation, a community trauma that was clearly not resolved.[216] Eighty years later, it was a deeply buried wound, a racial atrocity hidden in plain sight, so wrapped in secrecy that Hilliard-Nunn had to patiently pick out the names and family connections of the victims with the same painstaking effort with which the miners once extracted phosphate in the old pits.

Hilliard-Nunn was concerned that the history would be forever lost, and in 2002, organized the first official memorial service for

---

215   ibid
216   Claudia Aiden, *Gainesville Sun*, "The Newberry Six," September 4, 2005

the Newberry lynching victims, under the canopy of the remnant of the oak grove at the old picnic grounds that in early days was called Hangman's Island, and since 1916, Lynch Hammock. Fifty guests, including descendants of the victims of the nearby Rosewood Massacre, gathered to tell their stories and speak their names, breaking the oath of silence on the very ground where it was originally made.

Hilliard-Nunn was a force in local historic preservation in Alachua County, and her continued focus on the Newberry lynching encouraged more investigative journalists to study the nearly lost history. In 2005, African-American journalist Claudia Adrien revisited the lynching in an in-depth piece that appeared in the *Gainesville Sun*. Though several of James Dennis' grandchildren were still living in the Jonesville area, they were elderly and refused to discuss the event on the record.

Aiden wrote, "The granddaughter of Jim Dennis, one of those murdered, stands in her living room in defiance. Her blue-gray eyes, a stark contrast to her brown skin, peer through the large lenses of her glasses. The Black woman, somewhere in her 80s, cannot forget what has haunted her family for almost 90 years—though she isn't ready to reveal anything and insists that her name not be used for this article. 'I don't want to talk about that,' declares the elder Dennis, her voice shaking."[217]

The reluctance of the community to speak about the lynching was still common on both sides of the racial divide. Billy Barry, Jr., whose father had gone on the record to speak in 1977, denied Newberry's complicity completely, insisting, "It wasn't a community mishap. It was done by a few people."[218]

His answer can be read as literal denial, or more likely as a bit of revision to the Sachs interview of 1977, where Frank Dudley had widened the mob to two hundred of the "best men in the district," thus

---

217   Claudia Adrien, *Gainesville Sun*, "The Newberry Six," September 4, 2005
218   ibid

making it sound as if all of Newberry had been in the hammock for the actual lynching. Barry, who was a precise man, was challenging that assumption, pointing out that a handful of men—the men in the automobiles, who were Deputy Wynne's closest friends, who'd shot James Dennis in cold blood, and abducted Long's family—were the most complicit.

There was a kernel of hard truth in his answer. There was also an enormous gap of unspoken information that a Newberry native of his generation could have passed on—oral history, and second-hand—but valuable and insightful, had he chosen to cross the line.

He chose not, which was surely a missed opportunity, as by 2005 nearly all of the first-source witnesses had passed, with the West End of Alachua County feeling the pressure of West Gainesville's explosive growth. By the time Highway 26 was widened to four lanes at the turn of the millennium, the farmlands between Fort Clarke and Jonesville, including the old phosphate mines at Tioga, were well on their way to being converted to estate subdivisions with lush landscaping and wrought iron gates, and no mention of the convict labor that once sweated their banks.

The swelling population threatened to swallow any remembrance of the lynching, which was no longer locked in secrecy but still hardly a welcome conversation piece in an area of sudden affluence. The extensive renovation and preservation at the Dudley State Park seemed enough history for anybody, though the quiet work of digging up the connection of the Dudley family and the lynching continued.

***

In attendance at the 2002 memorial was a Black historian from Miami, Dr. Marvin Dunn. A native of Deland, Florida, Dunn was born into the Jim Crow system and witnessed discrimination and racial threat. An educator and professor of psychology at FIU, he wrote about the Black experience in Miami, and did on-the-ground research at the sites of past racial violence in research for an upcoming book.[219]

Dunn had two photographs of lynch mobs in his possession that he'd found many years before in the bowels of the basement of the Jacksonville Public Library. The photographs were labeled "Lake City," and long presumed to be of the Lake City Massacre of 1911.

Dunn suspected the photographs were of the Newberry lynching and began visiting the area for confirmation. He spoke to descendants of the lynching victims, and after several investigative visits to Newberry, presented an enlarged photograph of the mob to the rangers at the Dudley State Park, who identified three of the four Dudley brothers.

While Dr. Dunn was doing his cross-Florida investigation, Dr. Hilliard-Nunn continued her local work documenting the oral histories of the Black farmers of Jonesville. A candle-lighting ceremony to honor the victims had been held at Pleasant Plain in 1916, and in 2019, after a long collaboration with the descendants of the Dennis, McHenry, Long and Young families, a permanent state historic marker was erected there, at the emotional heart of Black Jonesville.

An esteemed visitor at the event was Newberry Mayor Jordan Marlowe, a history teacher by profession, who took the podium and offered that thing that had never been done in Black Jonesville—an apology.

"Good afternoon and welcome," he told the assembled crowd, some of whom were descendants of the Dennis, Young, Long and McHenry families. "My name is Jordan Marlowe, and I am the mayor of the City of Newberry. I really can't tell you how honored I am to be here today. I feel so small to be a part of such an important moment in our history, to be a part of this moment in time. Every single one of you here today, I want you to take this moment and think about what is about to happen here, think about what you are about to witness, what you are now, and will forever in the pages of history, be a part of.

---

219   Marvin Dunn, *A History of Florida Through Black Eyes*, 2016

"The weight of this moment, and the realization that I, like you, get to be a part of it, it fills me with pride. There are moments, where, if we stop and listen, we can hear the footsteps of God, and then we know we are engaged in the work of the righteous.

"This moment has been made possible by the work of others, and I am so grateful to them. I am grateful for their work. I am grateful for their commitment to the truth. I am grateful for their commitment to ensuring that our children, my children, will not grow up in world too frightened to speak the truth, not too frightened to face the truth, and one day, one day, not too frightened to apologize for that truth.

"And, in fact, that day, that day is this day. For, as Martin Luther King, Jr. said, 'The time is always right to do what is right.' And the truth is, I am sorry. We are here to recognize that six people were murdered, were murdered without trial, without justice, without compassion, and I am sorry that we, as a society, failed them. And they deserve, their memory deserves, their families deserve, their descendants deserve an apology, and today, I stand before you, and I say, as God is my witness, I am sorry."

He went on to read an official Proclamation of the City of Newberry, Florida:

WHEREAS on August 18th 1916, six innocent people: Jim Dennis, Bert Dennis, Mary Dennis, Stella Young, Andrew McHenry, and Reverend Josh J. Baskins were murdered;

WHEREAS on October 27th 1916, Boisy Long, after being found guilty by an all-white jury, who took a total of seven minutes to deliberate his case, was executed;

WHEREAS the City of Newberry acknowledges that nowhere in the course of these events was justice to be found;

WHEREAS the City of Newberry acknowledges that a sacred duty of any society, a sacred duty of any community, is to protect the innocent, and this dark moment represents a failure of society and a failure of community;

WHEREAS the City of Newberry acknowledges the truth, that lynching was a common practice, that lynching was immoral, and that lynching was used to terrorize African-Americans not just here in our community but across our Nation;

WHEREAS the City of Newberry recognizes value in recalling the role that our community played in the history of racial injustice and in taking steps for reconciliation;

WHEREAS the City of Newberry citizens have participated with City and County officials in an effort to bring attention to events in Newberry's past, which must be understood as an essential step towards genuine and sincere reconciliation;

WHEREAS the City of Newberry recognizes that this historical marker will, and should, serve both as a reminder of the sins of the past and as a symbol of the desire to move forward together in openness, honesty, fairness, and unity, but most importantly in truth;

NOW, THEREFORE, be it resolved that by virtue of the authority vested in me as Mayor of the City of Newberry, I do hereby proclaim the events of August 18th 1916, commonly known as the Newberry Six, as the darkest moment in our community's past. Further, I do hereby proclaim the actions taken that day as a failure of our community to do unto others as they'd have done unto them. May this marker shine a light on our sins so that we may repent of them. And, may the sincerity of our regret serve as a reminder to never again descend into the darkness of hatred and bigotry.

IN WITNESS WHEREOF, I have hereto set my hand and caused the Great Seal of the City of Newberry, Florida to be affixed in Newberry, Florida, this 27th day of April, in the year two thousand and nineteen.

Honorable Jordan Marlowe, Mayor

The audience of largely elderly citizens was visibly moved by his words and sincerity, as well they might. The official apology was 102 years in the making.

But it was a sincere apology, from one community to another, and there are plans afoot for a soil gathering service in collaboration with the Equal Justice Initiative. Six to eight mason jars of soil from beneath the oaks at Lynch Hammock will be placed in the museum in Montgomery, alongside the soil of other hammocks, from crossroads and hamlets across the South. The stories of the lynchings that took place on the soil will be recorded along with their stories, so that they aren't lost to memory.

Such is the natural beauty of the old church grounds at Pleasant Plain that the threat of annihilation by gentrification will likely be its next battle. For the moment, the quiet rural corner of the old West End looks much as it did in 1916: a low-slung white church with a belfry before and a graveyard behind, overhung with moss-draped laurel and live oak that cover the property with a close, calming canopy.

Figure 33. Pleasant Plain Methodist Church

The church was not shuttered by the violence of 1916, or the World Wars after, but has been in continuous service since it was founded by former enslaved laborers in 1866, when for a brief, bright moment, equality for all Americans seemed within reach. It is a fitting home for the memorial, which not only marks a painful epoch in history, but stands as evidence of Pleasant Plain's faithfulness, and the tenacity of the Black Jonesville farmers who have held their space there for more than 150 years.

Figure 34. Memorial at Pleasant Plain

The memorial itself cannot undo the evil of August 18 and 19, 1916. The dead will remain dead. But they now have a voice, a permanent reminder of not only their unjust deaths, but an indication of who they were in life; as farmers and as family: daughter, sister, mother; brother, son, friend. Their time on earth is over, but they will never be silenced again.

Chapter Twelve

EVENTUAL ENDINGS

The **Reverend William Young**, the patriarch of the Young and McHenry family, and father of Stella Young and Andrew McHenry, lost his wife Della only two years after the lynching, on October 18, 1918, in Newberry when she was fifty-one. They had been married twenty-three years. Two years later, on the 1920 census, William Young could be found living in Gainesville on Thomas Street with his children, who were enrolled in school there. When Young died in 1933, his children returned him to Jonesville, to be buried next to his wife at Pleasant Plain.

Figure 35. Della Young's Grave, Pleasant Plain

Stella Young and Boisy Long's youngest child, **Murray Randolph**, who went on the record to speak of the lynching in 1977, was raised by his Aunt Julia, James Dennis' widow. He grew up on her farm, and served in the US Army as a mechanic. When his service was up, he returned to Newberry and worked at the John Deere tractor dealership. Randolph died in 1992 and is buried with his family at Pleasant Plain.

Figure 36. William Young's grave, Pleasant Plain

Randolph's Aunt Julia Dennis, who was left to retrieve her husband's body that bloody Friday morning, continued to live in the Jonesville area after the lynching. On the 1920 census, she was a thirty-three-year-old widow, raising ten children—her own three and seven who were orphaned by the lynching. When she died in 1974, Julia Dennis was buried with her husband at Pleasant Plain, along with his brothers and sisters, and sister-in-law. Her children put a tombstone of some distinction on her grave, with a photograph of her that gazes out, firm and clear-eyed.

Figure 37. Julia Dennis' Tombstone, Pleasant Plain

She and **James Dennis'** children have continued to defend their family homes and farms, not against racial violence, but gentrification. In 2002, a developer bought property inside the boundaries of the historic Black community in Jonesville, and proposed to close a historic road. In a rare public statement, the Dennis and Long families objected strenuously, Eunice Myers speaking for the family when she said, "We just don't want that kind of stuff out here. We've been out here for a long time, and it's been our place, and we just want to be left alone."[220]

Myers mentioned in an aside that people had been trying to run her family off the land since her grandmother, Julia Dennis, first moved here in the late 1800s. But the family has remained, even after Dennis' husband was lynched by a white gang in 1918. "I've gotten some good offers, but I could never sell," Myers said.[221]

Annie Dennis, **Gilbert Dennis'** widow, moved to Tarpon Springs, Florida, where she was living with her daughter on the 1930 census. She died in 1932.

J. J. Baskins' wife and three daughters stayed in Jonesville for a few years after his murder. They appeared on the 1920 census as farm labor, and eventually moved to Broward County, where Ellen Baskins lived with a daughter until her death, her occupation listed as a laundress.

Baskins' brother continued to farm in Newberry until his death, and J. J. Baskins has descendants in the area who attend memorials in his memory.

William Berry, Sr. owned a pharmacy for many years in Newberry, and was active in every aspect of the community's life. He made his mark in Florida agriculture when he developed a cure for screw worms, which he manufactured in a small building in downtown Newberry. He and his son Billy were active in historic

---

220   Tim Lockette, "An Unpaved Future," *Gainesville Sun*, December 19, 2002
221   ibid

preservation. They donated many family photographs to the state, and can be viewed online at *The Florida Memory Project.*

Sheriff P. G. Ramsey was elected to three terms as sheriff, from 1909 till 1924. He served as president of the Florida Sheriff's Association from 1923 until 24. He died in 1933, in Gainesville.

Deputy Tom Mobley returned to his native Suwannee County shortly after the lynching. On his World War I draft card, signed the year after the lynching, he was not listed as a deputy by profession, but a farmer. He died in Live Oak in 1940.

Lemuel Harris and his family moved to Pinellas County in 1928, for economic reasons, as Newberry no longer had the population to support multiple pharmacists. Harris himself was not known to have ever discussed his shooting, though his son, late in his life, related a version of the story that Harris had been shot by an escaping prison inmate.

J. A. "Dixie" Jones farmed in Jonesville, and owned a construction company until his death in 1946. He is buried at Jonesville Baptist.

Grady Blount owned a gas station in Newberry for several years. He eventually moved to Gainesville, then Plant City, where he died in 1953.

Dr. Lester Weeks moved to Trenton in the late 1920s, and practiced medicine there until his death in 1937.

Dr. Samuel Getzen, who was reported as ill in the days after the lynching,[222] recovered and remained in Newberry, where he was a physician until his death in 1946.

---

222   *Tampa Tribune*, August 21, 1916

Dr. Joseph Ruff moved to Clearwater immediately after the lynching, where he died in 1936.

Deputy George W. Livingston was listed as a building contractor on the 1920 census. He died in Newberry in 1934.

Deputy W. Bruton moved to Micanopy by 1930, where he continued to work as a sheriff's deputy, and farmed.

Deputy Charles Pinkoson became a City Marshall in Gainesville shortly after the lynching. In 1924 he was elected Sheriff of Alachua County, narrowly beating the incumbent, P. G. Ramsey. He served one term, until 1928, when he was beaten by Robert Wells.

Deputy Robert J. Wells beat Sheriff Ramsey and Deputy Pinkoson in a close race for Alachua County Sheriff in 1929. He held it for one term, from 1929 to 1933, and would eventually serve as Gainesville police chief. He died in 1962 in Alachua.

Reason Edgar "Dick" Wright, who was a nephew of George Wynne, took over the job of town constable/deputy sheriff when his uncle was killed, in honor of Wynne. He held the position for fifteen years, then moved to Marion County to take a position in law enforcement there. Wright returned to Newberry on the twentieth anniversary of the lynching. On August 18, 1936, he was shot in the face by the deputy who had replaced him, H. C. Beard, on Main Street, in full view of fifteen witnesses.

The dispute between the men was said to have been over hog stealing. Beard was rumored to be part of a hog-stealing ring. Beard claimed Wright had threatened to kill him the next time he saw him, and had pulled first, though witnesses testified that Wright was unarmed. Beard stood trial and was found guilty of manslaughter. He was sentenced to ten years in Florida state prison, but was free by 1943 and working for J. A. Jones Construction on his WWII induction papers.

Squire Jackson was an influential farmer, preacher and healer in the Bennington area until his death in 1948. His son, Squire, Jr., died the year before. Both father and son are buried in the Greater Fort Clarke Missionary Baptist Cemetery.

Sidney J. Catts was inaugurated in January, 1917 as the twenty-second governor of Florida. He served a single term that was marked by controversy and multiple charges of corruption. He was an influential voice in Florida politics until his death in 1936, but never held political office again.

***

A few of the landmarks from 1916 still survive in the Jonesville/ Newberry area. The old jail in Newberry, where the lynching victims may have been held, is next to the historic light plant, on NW 260th Street in Newberry, where the city now stores equipment. The area is surrounded by a security fence and not open to the public, though historians wanting to see the jail can make inquiries of the city.

The actual lynching tree—a large live oak—was removed when Highway 235 was built there in the 1940s. It stood in a shallow sink at the corner of Highway 26A (Newberry Lane) and 235, a block northeast of Hitchcock's grocery. There is a slight rise of the ground on the east side of the intersection that marks the east lip of the natural amphitheater where political speeches were made, where the old oak stood.

The property is now privately owned, but many of the old oaks, remnants of the original hammock, can be easily seen from either Highway 26 or 235.

A portion of the old Gainesville Road can be seen directly in front of the Dudley homestead, where it crosses the old Jonesville Road.

Figure 38. The Old Gainesville Road at Dudley

The crossroads is inside The Dudley Farm State Park, which is open year-round, and provides a window into life at a turn-of-the-century North Florida farm.

Park rangers will discuss the Dudley family and its participation with the lynching of 1916, if requested. According to the park's map, George Wynne lived directly behind the homestead in an area that is now pasture, and not open to the public trails.

The kitchen where the lynching nooses were braided is on the homestead, and open to the public, at least to peer in the windows. The Dudley house where George Wynne spent most of his life, is open to the public. The upstairs, where his terrified nieces crept to get a glimpse of the gathering mob, is not.

Most of the Dudley family is buried at the cedar-dotted cemetery at Jonesville Baptist Church, as are other people associated with the weekend. A few are buried in the Newberry Municipal Cemetery, on the high ground north of the flagpole.

Most, if not all, of the Newberry lynching victims are buried at the cemetery at Pleasant Plain Methodist Church, where the memorial stands.

Also buried at Pleasant Plain is Dr. Patricia Hilliard-Nunn, who passed on August 5, 2020 after a long illness. She was active in reclaiming the Newberry and Jonesville history until the last week of her life, when she penned the text of the Newberry memorial. She requested she be buried under the oak canopy of the cemetery at Pleasant Plain, within forty feet of the graves of the Reverend Baskins and his wife, and most, if not all, of the lynching victims.

STUMBLING UPON STORY

W hen I was an undergraduate at the University of
Florida, I studied oral history with the inimitable Civil
Rights and Disabled Rights activist James Haskins. A
Black son of Alabama, Haskins was a popular children's author, book
reviewer and biographer, who taught folklore and children's lit in the
same department as creative writing, though he had grave doubts
that writing could be actually taught. He believed that writers were
born, not made; and that more often than not, they didn't pursue
stories, but stumbled upon them.

Nowhere in my life have I found this truer than when I stumbled
upon the tragic story of the Newberry mass lynching when I moved
to downtown Newberry in 1987. I was a young mother with three
small children, and a husband who worked nights. I was a fledgling
writer, with a degree in English and minor in Southern history from
UF that seemed practically worthless at the time, but did lend me an
appreciation of small town life in Newberry, circa 1987.

The old town reminded me of the neighborhood of my birth, on
the Westend of Marianna, an antebellum hamlet on the Alabama
side of the Florida panhandle where my mother was raised, and my
grandmother lived until her death in 1981. Newberry was smaller

than Marianna and far more modest, historically and architecturally speaking, but carried a scent of the old South that was immediately familiar—the hospitality of neighbors, the centrality of church life, and comforting blur between rural and city life. The local high school, two blocks away, provided all the sights and glorious drum sounds of high school sports, and still kept a few odd cows and donkeys on the property. The sound of roosters crowing in the morning was more commonplace than that of traffic. We technically lived in the downtown, but in 1987, downtown Newberry was still mighty country.

The house we bought was a tiny Cracker vernacular built in 1910 at the peak of the North Florida hard-rock phosphate boom. Originally a foursquare Georgian, the house had been renovated so thoroughly that the only original features were the brick fireplaces, the heart pine floors, and a ghost who used to walk the floors some nights that I'd hear when I was in bed, right on the edge of sleep.

When I mentioned the ghost to an eighty-two-year-old neighbor, Miss Katie Bea, she didn't question the matter, but only tried to remember the name of the family who built the house. She'd lived in her own house across the street for her entire life and knew everyone's old history. She thought our house had been built by the Hamiltons, and reminded me that people used to have funerals at home. She reckoned the ghost was someone who died there and couldn't quite shake free this mortal coil, and to me, that explanation was as good as any.

I didn't put any thought into exorcism or really overthink the spooky footsteps. In the South, restless ghosts are a reality, not as terrifying as they are a nuisance. They don't fly through the air like poltergeists, or shake the windows like haints, but tip-tap around the edge of consciousness, like mice in the floorboards, leaving tiny clues for sympathetic humans with discerning eyes.

Our neighborhood in the downtown was leafy, fading, and a little ramshackle, full of feral cats and interesting, half-dilapidated houses as old, and older, than our own, several too far gone for anyone to invest in their restoration. Newberry was not trending in the gentrification market back then. It was stiffly independent of the artsy, hip county seat at Gainesville, where the University of Florida and its hospitals supplied many local jobs. Newberrians were content to commute a half hour east every morning, along the two-lane Highway 26 that was all fields and woods and listing old tobacco barns, the unincorporated town of Jonesville unmarked and largely unnoticed, nothing more than a scattering of country churches, a bar and a feed store.

Neither Newberry nor Jonesville had much truck in the larger county. The money that could be had was in the hands of a few large-scale melon farmers and cattle ranchers, along with a handful of families who'd been there since the phosphate boom and still owned a piece of the bank. They remembered the glory days when the mines were open and the downtown was full of saloons, shootouts, and a women's dress store called Goodbreads featuring a sofa in the middle of the store where customers would recline, like Roman emperors, while salesladies brought out dresses for their inspection.

They recalled a different Newberry—a burgeoning brick town with an opera house, a theatre, several boarding houses and the high-end Florida Hotel, where drummers and phosphate managers ate their breakfast off china while reading the *New York Times*, then stepped out on the veranda for a cigar before starting their day. Passenger trains made regular stops at the downtown depot, as did the circus train, the brightly painted cars and cages of roaring lions drawing crowds of barefoot country children who'd run alongside, waving sticks and shouting.

I heard these stories from my neighbors, who were all elderly, most of them farm wives who'd moved to town when they were widowed, who'd let their children take over the family farm. A few were born and raised in genteel ease, with maids and nannies and chintz sofas, in a Southern life common at the time all over the South:

piano lessons, and summer trips to Cashiers; college at Bessie Tufts, and courting beaus on a front porch swing. These were the daughters of the town's founders who attended the same church their entire lives, and still had a bit of the old boom money, and were Cracker-cautious in spending it. They lived in turn-of-the-century family homes, drove aging Cadillacs, and had their hair done at the beauty shop a block away in the old brick-front downtown. Civic-minded and socially inclined, they insisted I join the local garden club, where I was the youngest member by fifty years.

An especial friend was Miss Katie Bea Cooke, who had lived in the same house her entire life and was a fount of history spanning an entire century. I have always loved to hear the stories of my elders, and when my children were settled for the night, I'd often cross our yards for a visit. Though Katie Bea was a charter member of First Baptist (also across the street), she kept wine in her house (awful Kmart wine) and wasn't above quietly sipping Jim Beam, which she called Jim *Bean.* When any of her many male relatives visited, she would disappear into her pantry under the stairs and emerge with a little glass that she would hand them without a word.

It made for good conversation, and she and I and whoever might stop in to join us talked about everything under the sun. Her cousin Doc Berry, who was well up in his nineties, and his son Billy, then in his late seventies, would often join us, their take on small town life a novel in itself.

At UF, I wrote—or tried to write—a paper about the notorious lynching of Claude Neale that took place in 1934 in northern Jackson County. I had heard it spoken about openly as a child, but when I started asking questions on the record, my sources dried up, seemingly overnight. I ended up writing a paper that included a mention of the lynching, but contained nothing new or extraordinary. I was a novelist, not an investigative journalist, and had none of the doggedness that was required to extract the painful, deeply buried racial secrets in the South.

I knew, vaguely, that there was a lynching in Newberry's history, way back, that included women, one of them pregnant. It was impossible not to know, because the last curve into town where you'd give people directions to your house, was called Lynch Hammock. I don't remember registering any particular unease when using the term. My family's roots in the South stretched to the early 1700s, and because of my father's job, we'd moved around a bit when I was a child, to New Orleans, Wiggins, Mississippi, Hattiesburg Mississippi, and a decade in Ocala, before I married and moved to Gainesville.

I had never lived in a town *without* a lynching history, and though my Newberry neighbors and I talked about everything else under the sun, and even organized a historic committee to celebrate Newberry's Centennial, the Newberry lynching had no part in it, a choice that seemed mutual on both sides of the tracks. I use the term literally, as Newberry was still physically segregated by the railroad tracks, with whites to the south and west, and Black Newberry northeast.

The segregation was by 1990 not hard and fast, as the town was so small that there were many friendships across the color lines. Our mayor, Freddie Warmack, was Black, and our children attended public schools together. My husband and our children attended an integrated church in Gainesville, which specifically preached against the evils of white supremacy and racial bias. Black men and women were in positions of leadership, including some who were natives of the West End of the County.

We were church friends of the sort that prayed with each other, ate with each other, and shared our toughest life challenges, and though we deplored racism in general and considered it a mortal sin, we never broached the subject of lynching. It was too complex, too painful. Once, at a night of prayer and testimony at our church, a well-meaning Northern lady took the stage to apologize to the Black people in the church for racism. The children of the South in the room did not react, either Black or white, with a blink or a tear, because there was a hard line of silence around the most dreadful episodes of racial violence that pretty much *had* to be ignored, if everyone was going to keep loving one another as Christ loved the Church.

Having it brought up in public that way was not only awkward, but it was *embarrassing*. We were all brothers and sisters in the Lord, and outside of that, brothers and sisters of the family of the South—a sprawling, multi-colored, cornbread-cooking, barbecue-loving family with a three-ton elephant in the room; a secret sunk in shame.

Everyone knew horror stories about atrocities that happened in the past— sometimes the not-so-distant past. But you didn't just stand up in church and *talk* about them, unless you *really* knew what you were talking about, and where the Newberry lynching was concerned, nobody really did. Offering a two-sentence apology, even at church, in the heat of testimony time, seemed tone-deaf and inadequate. As if an *apology* by an *outsider* would fix anything.

***

So we played nice and kept in our lanes, and when white neighbors in Newberry mentioned the lynching at all, vaguely, without personal reveal, I'd listen with as much interest as I did with any other piece of local history. My response, like as not, would be to comment that *whatever* happened in Newberry could never be as bad as the Claude Neal lynching, as if lynchings were a town sport, and *their* horrible horrors would never hold a candle to *our* horrible horrors.

It was a strange mindset.

Only on a few occasions, in moments of unguarded honesty, did any of my Newberry friends speak frankly of the lynching, and share family history. Once, on a fishing trip at the mouth of the Suwannee, a friend who'd lived in Newberry his entire life, and was then a city commissioner, recalled the lynching. His father was one of the teenagers who'd followed along in the trees, who got caught and were made to touch the rope. He didn't tell the story with huge gusto or shock; he didn't have to. We were all Southerners and had heard such stories our entire lives.

Another neighbor, Miss Essie Neagle, who made Easter baskets for neighboring children, was George Wynne's sister-in-law. She spoke a little of the lynching and would have spoken a great deal more if Katie Bea hadn't put such a stinkeye on her that she relented and moved on to other subjects.

Katie Bea steered well clear of the subject, though we often talked about local history. On one single occasion, an evening in the mid-1990s, I must have mentioned the Neale lynching, as she asked me when it happened.

When I told her "1934," she was surprised to hear lynchings were still being done that late in Florida history. I knew very little about the Newberry lynching and asked her when it happened.

"1916," she said, and after a long pause, offered that her uncle, Henry Tucker, who built the house where we were sitting, had driven Deputy Wynne to the train in that last-ditch effort to get him to a surgeon in Jacksonville.

Katie Bea, who was age six in 1916, and might very well have been one of the children who visited the hammock while the bodies were displayed, never spoke of that part of it. She just recalled, in a quiet voice, her uncle's account of driving Wynne down the bumpy lime rock Gainesville Road at breakneck speed, desperate to save his life.

She said that Wynne had regained consciousness long enough to raise up in the back seat and remind her uncle that the gates to the University of Florida, which were locked at ten in the evening, would block their way to the depot in Gainesville.

She said those were Wynne's last words, "The gates will be locked," before he lost consciousness and fell back on the seat.

I remember repeating, "The gates will be locked," and commenting that it was a hell of a last line, which she agreed.

And that was it.

Fifteen years later, after I'd published several novels and a cookbook, I decided to revisit the enigma of my family's racial history, in a novel, *American Ghost*. Katie Bea was gone by then, as were all the old Newberrians who'd served on the historic and beautification committees with me. I wrote the story in novel form because I believed that was the only way such stories would ever be told.

I knocked it out as best I could, inserting a few snippets of oral history that I thought strengthened the story, but keeping it strictly fiction, well off the holy ground of history. Telling that version was now impossible, I thought. The first-source witnesses were gone and everyone was tired of talking about all the old horror stories, anyway. We had a Black president and went to integrated churches and our children dated and married interracially. Racial atrocity was part of our American history, but not notably a fear for the future. In the words of Murray Randolph, what's done was done.

Except it wasn't.

While I was waiting that year-long wait that comes between finishing a novel and its launch, my daughter called me from work one day to tell me she'd come upon the strangest thing, a short video about the Newberry lynching. "There's a mob photo," she said.

I was amazed such a document existed and followed the link she sent taking me to a YouTube video, which featured a Black historian from Miami, Dr. Marvin Dunn, who did indeed have a photograph of what appeared to be a mob. The glimpse in the video was brief, but it did make me curious. Mob photographs are a tricky proposition in the South. I've had people—honest, frank people—tell me that far more of them exist in private hands than are ever displayed in public. Families sometimes just throw them out when they find them in estates, or give them to people who collect them—not just photos, but post cards, and even grisly souvenirs: sections of rope or, in the case of Claude Neal, a finger or toe kept in alcohol in a bottle (two of which still exist, in private hands in Marianna).

I was eventually able to track down Dr. Dunn, who turned out to be a retired psychology professor from Florida International University who grew up in Florida under the relentless injustice of Jim Crow. He has made it his mission to unearth the whitewashed racial violence that was a prominent, if rarely discussed, feature of early life in the Sunshine State.

When I told him I'd like to see the Newberry mob photograph, he offered to bring it to me. I had no idea where he lived at that time, and I learned that to show me the photograph he had to drive six hours from Miami.

It made for one of the strangest moments of my life, and no doubt of Dr. Dunn's, as we had moved out of downtown Newberry by then to a house in rural Jonesville, so far back in the woods that it isn't visible from the road, but seven acres into a closed canopy forest, with a listing tobacco barn to the left for a compass. Dunn couldn't have been sure of his welcome, as my cookbook was a celebration of Cracker Florida called *The Cracker Kitchen,* and my accent sounds like I grew up in a convict camp myself. For him to jump in his car in Coral Gables and drive into the wilds of North Florida, to show a self-described Florida Cracker a lynching photo—that's a man serious in his work.

It didn't take too much nerve on my part; I was just curious. Without much ado, Dr. Dunn came to the house the next day and after a few pleasantries, slid the mob photograph from an envelope onto an ottoman in my living room. I don't remember my exact reaction, possibly stark silence, because the photograph, enlarged for detail, was shocking in every sense of the word.

The strewn corpses were shocking, as were the smiling faces of the mob. The fact that I recognized a few of them was not good at all, especially because one of the younger faces was surely, surely, that of my old friend Doc Berry. He and Billy were both slight men who had a characteristic way of standing with their hip hitched to one side. Even more startling were the Dudley brothers—all four of them. Of course! Deputy Wynne was their uncle.

There have only been a few times in my life that I have been literally speechless, and that was one of them. Dunn knew I recognized some faces; it was obvious by my reaction. My familiarity with Dudley was thanks to my membership on the Newberry historic committee in the early 1990s, which supported and celebrated Myrtle Dudley's great gift to the state.

Back in the 1990s Jonesville was nothing more than a bar, a blinking light and a feed store, and Dudley a backroads jungle, the entire property overgrown so completely you could barely make out the bones of the farm. At historic or social occasions, Myrtle herself would greet you from her wheelchair on the ramshackle porch, and if you were polite enough, would offer a hand, and tell you a tale or two, or at least nod while one of the attendant rangers told the tale. The Newberry Garden Club had a few events there, always made lively by a handful of barred-rock roosters who would chase hens while a gloved and hatted guest speaker tried to talk about native plants.

Billy Barry was a huge supporter of the state park, and sold (or bartered; we never knew) some of his own farmland to extend the park by seventy acres. On one of the first public days, he walked me around the property and showed me where the ponds once were, as well as the remnants of the crossroads of the old Gainesville and Jonesville roads.

His family then owned the Jones property across the highway and he took me on a tour of those buildings, too, which he sadly noted were not as well-preserved. The Dudleys had built their farm buildings on stone foundations. Their Jones cousins had not, and their tobacco barns were not fit for reclamation, he thought. Indeed, except for a single structure that was moved across the highway to the State Park, they are long demolished, the flowering plum trees the only sign of J. J. Jones antebellum homestead.

Katie Bea, who was a walking encyclopedia where local history was concerned, was never very enthused with the reclamation of Dudley Farm. Once, at a garden club event there, when I saw Myrtle on the porch and proposed we speak to her, Katie Bea replied dryly, "Oh, I know Myrtle," and refused to go up the walk to pay homage.

She waited by the gate and when I returned, commented that when she was a child, one of the Dudley sisters had been a substitute teacher at the old schoolhouse in Newberry, and had given her a whipping. "She made a good job of it," Katie Bea commented shortly.

She was not alone in her measured response to the statewide celebration that surrounded the great coup of Myrtle donating the family farm. Black Jonesvillians, whose families had farmed the area since Reconstruction, watched the State of Florida's extensive and expensive refurbishment of Dudley with a very measured side-eye, especially the museum and walking tours where, in the early days, the individual members of the Dudley family were celebrated with Disney-like enthusiasm. The farm mare was named Dollie, after a Dudley daughter; the mule was Fred, after Fred Wynne. There were roses named for daughters, and excerpts from the Captain's letters on display, all presenting the Dudley family as prototypes of the East Florida Cracker, famous for their work ethic, their independence, and above all, their Southern hospitality.

Black history was included in the park's celebration of early farm life in limited ways, such as on Plow Days and at cane grindings, when a handful of Black Jonesville farmers, including Lyman Long, demonstrated how to plow rows with mules, straight as a plumb line. The farm's genesis as a slave plantation was glossed over, as was P. B. H. Dudley's early years as an overseer and slave trader.

The Black labor that was essential to the operation of the farm was praised, but there was very little exploration into the inescapable fact that members of the Dudley family were without a doubt participant, and very likely ringleaders, in the racial violence that frequently swept the West End post-Reconstruction. The state could not claim ignorance, because the public record was available, and certainly neither Frank nor Myrtle Dudley ever took pains to deny the racial hatred embedded in the family history.

The official Dudley biography, which was sold at the gift shop, included a chapter on the lynching, but it was written with a selectiveness that said everything and said nothing. The basic elements of the weekend were relayed, but the harsh racial invective in both Frank's interview and Myrtle's oral history was not only downplayed, but intentionally omitted.

The biography did include a photograph of the Dudley sons, and before I'd go so far as to identify a face in a mob photo, I needed some collaboration. I found my ten-year-old copy of the biography, and compared the faces of the Dudley sons and the men in the photograph. They were a match.

I have to confess that, even with the verification of the photographs in the Dudley biography, I hesitated to ID the photograph, at least for a few moments. I actually pretended to need to pee and left Dr. Dunn alone in the living room while I retired to the bathroom to take a breath and consider the implications. It suddenly seemed a foolish diversion, in a time of present-day violence and racial strife, to drag up a ninety-nine-year-old murder.

At that time, I had no idea that Myrtle Dudley had spoken of the lynching, and that Frank Dudley had done an interview back in '77 that was delivered to all of Newberry in a Sunday supplement. I thought I was the only person on earth who had connected the dots, and I wasn't happy to be in that position.

But what else could I do? It was true. I didn't know the details, and as Frank Dudley predicted, I almost certainly would *never* know them, not one hundred percent, in a sure and fast way, an incompleteness that momentarily paralyzed me.

But I did recognize the faces, and in the end, it was simple obedience to the Golden Rule that settled it—the sacred commandment to do unto others as you would have done unto you. There is no one on earth more curious and compelled than I am by my ancestors and my family history. If it was my grandmother, or grandfather, or cousins or uncles in that photograph, tossed in the dirt at the feet of a smug and satisfied mob, and someone could offer me a clue to the details of their death, I'd want to know.

So I told Dr. Dunn what little I knew and he soon left, with a long drive to Miami before him. Unbeknownst to me, he stopped at Dudley and showed the photo to a ranger, who identified three of the Dudley sons. Dr. Dunn stopped by to tell me on his way home, and I was relieved. To me, the only thing worse than identifying someone in a lynch-mob photograph would be *wrongly* identifying them.

I was not on the inside of the state's reaction to the find; indeed, I was far, far outside of it. My husband's job required us to move out of state for a few years, though we kept our house in Jonesville and often returned. I was in attendance when the staff at the Dudley State Park invited Dr. Dunn to speak, and thought it a sign of changing times—that the state was finally coming clean on the Dudley family history, though my optimism proved premature.

The next Plow Day I attended, members of the Citizen's Support Organization recognized and confronted me on the back porch in a way that would have been threatening if it hadn't been comic. An elderly white man who had been wonderfully friendly at Dr. Dunn's talk, became so agitated that he literally fell off the back steps of the Dudley house (fortunately into the arms of my son-in-law and daughter, who were witnessing it all from the yard, and caught him, preventing a nasty fall).

The lady who had welcomed Dr. Dunn to the park archives just months earlier was now dismissive. She stood on the corner of the back porch and openly complained that there was talk—to her, just absurd—of adding slave cabins to the Dudley farm complex.

When I tried to escape the conversation by saying that I was on my way to visit Fred (the mule), she coolly informed me that both Fred and Dollie (the mare) were dead. They'd escaped their paddock and been hit and killed by traffic on Highway 26. She hinted darkly that Dr. Dunn, or Black people in league with him, were responsible for their death, a comment that was as ludicrous as it sounds, but at the moment it shook me up. Fred was my pal.

I left the farm that day feeling like a Cracker Pandora, who'd opened a box of suffering and curse to no good end. I was still curious about all of it, and over the next few years, told many a fine investigative journalist and historian the bizarre tale of a Black family that had been lynched two miles from my house in 1916. I all but begged them to do the work and write the story.

No one took me up on it, and I continued to collect data, and track down the odd side-trail. I discovered the ongoing work of Patricia Hilliard-Nunn, a professor in African-American Studies at UF, who had stumbled upon the lynching much as I had, while doing research for a documentary she was making of the history of Black Alachua County. Many of the older citizens she interviewed alluded to their roots in Jonesville, and to the weekend in 1916 that had changed their lives, and indeed, the whole landscape of Alachua County.

Tricia began to study the lynching more carefully, but found the subject so taboo that it required patience and finesse to collect any new data. When she first began her work, some of Jim Dennis' children were yet alive. They were witnesses to his abduction and though one of his daughters spoke to her openly about it, when it came time to speak on film, she became so physically nervous that she could not go through with it.

In time, Tricia did find descendants of the victims who would speak to her, and even gather in public remembrance ceremonies, at Newberry and at Pleasant Plain. She continued to work with the City of Newberry, Alachua County and the State of Florida, pressing all ends to bring about a public memorial that was acceptable to the families of the descendants. The long-unfolding journey lasted for decades and culminated in the unveiling of the state memorial on April 27, 2019, which bore text that Tricia had written herself.

Tricia encouraged me to continue my research and offered invaluable access to her own knowledge of the event, culled from her many years in the field. She was several years my junior, but spoke with the unflappable calm of an elder when discussing the lynching and aftermath, and the complex racial landscape of the event.

I often found it overwhelming and tried to put it aside for other projects, but it wouldn't let itself stay on the shelf. Tricia and I both joked that the spirits out there in Jonesville were on our track, rattling our windows at night, wanting us to tell their story. When I was home in Florida, I took a few trips, so low-key I practically wore a fake beard, to walk Dudley Farm.

One holiday weekend in 2015, I was babysitting my toddler grandson and took him there to see the Cracker cows and stroll around. We were on the edge of summer in North Florida, and after an afternoon of hard rain, the farm was particularly lovely, all damp leaves and dappled sunshine; the enormous fig trees full of warm, ripe fruit, the smell taking me back as it always did to my grandfather's little farm in Marianna.

I no longer spoke to anyone at Dudley, and if any of the rangers or volunteers recognized me, they kept it to themselves, thus making for a serene visit for me, such as it had been in the early days with the garden club. I missed the simplicity of those days, when the rangers and volunteers were welcoming. As I buckled my grandson in his car seat, I was assaulted by a wave of pure regret. I wondered if all the hard feelings the mob photograph had aroused were necessary, or even helpful. Maybe I'd overworked this particular fixation to no good end; had just stirred to the pot, without the favor of the Lord.

As I backed out of the parking lot and headed for the park entrance, I worried that I might have developed a case of that most embarrassing of post-menopausal white-woman maladies—White Savior Complex. The very thought was disheartening, and I was rethinking all of it when I got to the end of the lane, to the stop sign at the main park gates on Highway 26.

I looked left for traffic, then right toward Newberry, where the state park sign, not twenty feet away, was set in big block letters for the Memorial Day weekend with a single word: REMEMBER.

Figure 39. Sign at Dudley State Park, May 2015

I did a double take when I saw it, and even pulled over to take a photo of it to commemorate the moment. Sometimes you look to God for a sign and do not get one. Sometimes you're not even looking, and get one anyway.

***

So I have remembered, and put it on paper along with sources and citations, in the hope that it will open up further conversation, and remembrance, and hold space at the table of history for the people who died the weekend of August 18 and 19, 1916 in Newberry/ Jonesville, Florida—who, had we lived in the same era, would have been my neighbors.

They are: James Dennis. His brother Gilbert, and sister Mary. His sister-in-law, Stella Young, and her brother Andrew McHenry. Their friend and neighbor, the Reverend J. J. Baskins.

I pray they rest in peace and rise in glory.

I pray it for us all.

SOURCES

*T*he *Crisis* magazine is the official publication of the National Association for the Advancement of Colored People (NAACP). It was founded in 1910 by W.E.B. Du Bois. *The Crisis* was the strongest voice against lynching in its day and sent seasoned investigative journalists South to investigate them. *The Crisis* archive, including the November 1916 issue, are available online at the Online Book Page https://onlinebooks.library.upenn.edu.

Myrtle Dudley's Oral History can be found at the Samuel Proctor Oral History Program Collection, P.K. Yonge Library of Florida History, University of Florida. It is available online for PDF download at https://ufdc.ufl.edu/UF00093314/00001/pdf.

Firsthand reporting on the Reconstruction Klan in Alachua County can be found online in searchable form under: *Report of the Joint Select Committee to Inquire into the Condition of Affairs in the Late Insurrectionary States, made to the two Houses of Congress* February 19, 1872

The Federal Census records were accessed via paid subscription at Ancestry.com.

Newspaper citations were found online via paid subscription at Newspapers.com, and from the Library of Congress, at https://chroniclingamerica.loc.gov/lccn/sn95047222/1916-08-19/ed-1/seq-1/.

Ron Sachs' investigation into the Newberry lynching, "Conspiracy of Silence Shrouds 1916 Lynching," appeared in the *Sunday Magazine*, an insert in the *Gainesville Sun*, on November 7, 1977.

Claudia Adrien's piece, "The Newberry Six" appeared in the *Gainesville Sun*, September 4, 2005

Tim Lockette's piece, "An Unpaved Future" appeared in the *Gainesville Sun*, December 19, 2002

BIBLIOGRAPHY

William Wilbanks, *Forgotten Heroes: Police Officers Killed in Early Florida, 1840-1925*, 1998

Ben Pinkard, with Sally Morris, *Dudley Farm, a History of Florida Farm Life*, Alachua Press, 2003

Lizzie PRB Jenkins, *Alachua County, Black American Series*, Arcadia Publishing

Marvin Dunn, *A History of Florida Through Black Eyes*, 2016

Wayne Flynt, *Cracker Messiah, Governor Sidney J. Catts of Florida*, 1977

Carl Webber, *Eden of the South*, Leve & Alden, 1883

Paul Ortiz, *Emancipation Betrayed, The Hidden History of Black Organizing and White Violence in Florida from Reconstruction to the Bloody Election of 1920*, University of California Press, 2005

Daniel L. Schafer, *Zephaniah Kingsley Jr. and the Atlantic World: Slave Trader, Plantation Owner, Emancipator* University of Florida Presses, 2013

William Warren Rogers, James M. Denham, *Florida Sheriffs: A History, 1821-1945,* (Sentry Press, 2001)

Larry E. Rivers, *Slavery in Florida: Territorial Days to Emancipation,* University Press of Florida, 2000)

Isabel Wilkerson, *The Warmth of Other Suns: The Epic Story of America's Great Migration,* Vintage, 2010

Dana Ste. Claire, *Cracker: Cracker Culture in Florida History,* University of Florida Press 2006

Photograph citation

The mob photographs are used with the permission of Dr. Marvin Dunn. All other photographs are courtesy of the Florida Memory Project, or from the author's collection.

CPSIA information can be obtained
at www.ICGtesting.com
Printed in the USA
LVHW030219200821
695686LV00006B/761